Skating for Gold

Robin Cousins

with Howard Bass

Skating for Gold

Stanley Paul

London Melbourne Sydney Auckland Johannesburg

also by Howard Bass

THE SENSE IN SPORT
THIS SKATING AGE
THE MAGIC OF SKIING
WINTER SPORTS
SUCCESS IN ICE SKATING
INTERNATIONAL ENCYCLOPAEDIA
OF WINTER SPORTS

LET'S GO SKATING
TACKLE SKATING
ICE SKATING FOR PLEASURE
ICE SKATING
THE LOVE OF SKATING
ELEGANCE ON ICE

Stanley Paul & Co. Ltd

An imprint of the Hutchinson Publishing Group

3 Fitzroy Square, London W1P 6JD

Hutchinson Group (Australia) Pty Ltd
30–32 Cremorne Street, Richmond South, Victoria 3121
PO Box 151, Broadway, New South Wales 2007

Hutchinson Group (NZ) Ltd
32–34 View Road, PO Box 40–086, Glenfield, Auckland 10

Hutchinson Group (SA) Pty Ltd
PO Box 337, Bergvlei 2012, South Africa

First published 1980
© Robin Cousins 1980

Set in Monotype Times

Printed in Great Britain by The Anchor Press Ltd
and bound by Wm Brendon & Son Ltd
both of Tiptree, Essex

British Library Cataloguing in Publication Data

Cousins, Robin
  Skating for gold.
  1. Cousins, Robin
  2. Skaters – Great Britain – Biography
  I. Title   II. Bass, Howard
  796.9'1'0924   GV850.C/

ISBN 0 09 143300 2

Contents

	PREFACE	9
1	A Dream Comes True	15
2	Handstands and Cartwheels	28
3	Delayed World Début	37
4	My First Olympics	44
5	Knee Deep in Trouble	53
6	Ice Time Problems	61
7	A Close Call	68
8	Touring and Reflecting	77
9	Music and Leisure	85
10	All Worthwhile	94
11	Living in the States	103
12	Que Será, Será	111
13	A Royal Honour	121
14	The Big Season Build-Up	131
15	Triple Crown Chance	143
	APPENDICES	
1	National and International Record	156
2	How the Judges Mark	157
3	Jumps and Their Values	158

To
Mum, Dad, Martin and
Nick

'One crowded hour of glorious life
is worth an age without a name.'
Thomas Osbert Mordaunt

Preface

When, in October, 1977, Robin Cousins surveyed his then best-ever figure tracings during the Skate Canada internationals at Moncton, New Brunswick, he said he wished he could have cut out the relevant piece of ice and shipped it home. He knew those etchings made by his well-controlled blades probably symbolized the turning point of his career.

Before the contest, this lanky six-footer told me how much he felt his technique in figures had advanced during summer training under Carlo Fassi at Denver, Colorado. He proceeded to prove it in no uncertain manner.

What a transformation this was from the worried young man with an injured knee in Tokyo the previous March to a newly confident and obviously fit skater, impatient to display his much improved skills.

Most of his earlier shortcomings in figures, particularly an urge to rush them through too quickly and therefore less accurately, had at last been eradicated.

He had learned to restrain previous incautious impulses so well that, henceforth, he was able to use superior jumping and spinning to forge ahead, rather than merely reduce an initial deficit.

The still-bashful Robin began to realize that the world title could be within his grasp. His enforced retirement during a courageous free skating effort in the Tokyo World Championships of 1977 came as no great surprise. The wonder was that he had managed to go so far, even to the point of including a triple toe loop jump in the earlier short programme.

After the opening two minutes of his longer free skating performance, that wretched left knee which had been troublesome for agonizing weeks again came out of place, as one had feared it might, yet somehow he still bravely completed a tortuous flying camel spin, in a desperate hope that it would force the knee back into place.

With hindsight, it appears the British Champion did himself more good at the time, by showing he could rate sixth even with such a tormented knee before the final free skating, than if he had opted not to compete at all. It had been a controversial decision.

Within a week after leaving Tokyo, he had the offending cartilage removed and, eight weeks later, was back on the ice practising triples. Two years previously, he had had a cartilage taken from the other knee and, thanks to expert medical handling, made a similarly rapid and complete recovery.

Was it possible that this dauntless human powerhouse could eventually emulate John Curry by becoming World, European and Olympic Champion? Was that rarely accomplished triple crown beyond his reach in 1980? If not, what a remarkable national achievement it would be for a second British skater to attain such dizzy heights within so short a span.

Until Curry's triumphs of 1976, the last time a Brit topped the winner's podium in an international championship had been in 1939. That year, Graham Sharp gained both World and European titles and probably would have enjoyed a lengthy spell at the top had not war intervened.

Thirty-seven years was a very long time to wait for a compatriot to follow suit, thereby sparking a national resurgence of interest in the sport. Britain's rink managers reported soaring attendance figures. Through television, the Curry example did for skating what Olga Korbut had done for gymnastics – and Cousins continued the momentum.

As happens to many sportsmen, Cousins got undeservedly muted publicity in 1976 while bettered by a headline-capturing fellow-countryman. Bettered, but hardly overshadowed. It was not too widely realized that, in December, 1975, just a few weeks before Curry's fifty-four days of international glory, Cousins frightened the life out of his soon-to-be-illustrious opponent in the British Championships at Richmond.

In that event, Cousins actually defeated Curry in the free skating, out-jumping and out-spinning the man whose days of international stardom were so soon to follow. Only higher marks for the earlier compulsory figures enabled Curry to scrape home and retain his national title by a marginal decision.

It is curious how one tiny impulsive action can transform the course of a life. It certainly did so in the case of Cousins. In 1965, at the age of eight, Robin was on a family seaside holiday at Bournemouth when, on a particularly hot August day, he and his mother ventured into the local ice rink simply because it looked 'somewhere cool to go'.

Robin had never watched skating before and, liking what he saw, he persuaded his mother to book a lesson with an instructor. Taking to the ice like the proverbial duck to water, the natural ability he displayed that day was sufficient to cause the coach to express astonishment that he had not worn a pair of skates before.

A year later, after a new rink opened near his Bristol home, Robin resolved to take up the sport seriously and Pamela Davies, the senior resident tutor, was engaged to take charge.

'Robin was a very keen pupil from the outset,' Pamela recalls. 'A real live-wire, he was very responsive to my teaching. We have the same artistic temperament and he is very musically minded.

'He showed so much potential, so I told him that one day he could be a champion if he listened and practised hard enough. I was very strict and he used to get very upset as he was a sensitive boy, but he knew it was for his own good.'

His style was jerky at first and growing quickly did not help, but gradually he started to acquire the necessary flow. Spinning came easily to him, but he always enjoyed jumping most of all.

Pam recalls: 'He used to throw himself into the air and not think about coming down. So we padded out his hips with foam rubber to lessen the bruises.'

Born into a sports-loving family in Bristol on 17 August 1957, Robin John Cousins is the youngest of three brothers whose parents enjoyed outdoor recreation. His father Fred, a motor car taxation officer, used to play soccer for Millwall, and his mother Jo was trained to swim the English Channel. Eldest brother Martin plays rugby and cricket and Nick, the middle one, is a school sports master.

Carefully prepared for proficiency tests, Robin took his first three on the same December day of 1967 – for figures, free skating and ice dancing – and passed the lot. He gained a dozen trophies before winning the British junior title in 1972, finishing third later the same year in his first national senior championship.

Fifteenth in his international début, at the European Championships in Cologne in 1973, and afterwards tenth in the first Skate Canada at Calgary, he was held back the following year by a chipped ankle bone. Eleventh in the 1974 European event at Zagreb with his ankle strapped, the aggravated injury compelled his withdrawal from the subsequent world contest in Munich, which was to have been his first.

In 1975, he again finished eleventh in the European at Copenhagen, twelfth in the World at Colorado Springs, and was close runner-up to the American, Charles Tickner, at Skate Safari in Johannesburg.

Then came the first cartilage operation but, two months after its removal, he was runner-up to Curry for the third successive time in the British Championship, confounding the critics by outpointing John in both sections of the free skating.

Curry's subsequent triple international victories quite naturally diverted much attention from Robin's continuing improvement in 1976 – sixth in the Geneva European, tenth in the Innsbruck Olympics (and the only competitor to land five triples) and ninth in the Gothenburg World Championships.

Since then, four easy British title wins, three European bronze medals, one

11

world silver medal, one world bronze medal and an ominous victory over Tickner in the Moncton Skate Canada added significantly to the record before becoming runner-up in the World Championships and European Champion in 1980 at Dortmund and Gothenburg respectively. The latter two accomplishments were, of course, almost dwarfed in most minds that season by his attainment at Lake Placid of the ultimate amateur goal, a cherished Olympic gold medal.

During the last three seasons of his amateur career, he won a supplementary gold medal as the best free skater in every championship he entered.

Don Jackson and Dick Button, the world's greatest skaters in earlier decades, share a particularly high regard for Robin's skating. Jackson enthuses: 'Britain was fortunate to have another highly accomplished skater so ready to take over the reins from Curry. His jumps and spins were so impressive that, by 1977, there was never any doubt in my mind that he would go right to the very top.'

Button says: 'Robin is my kind of jumper. He's not afraid, but keeps his cool and his spins are consistently reliable.'

The world's most experienced skating judge, Pam Davis (spelt with no 'e' and not to be confused with her instructing near-namesake) is renowned for prudence when offering praise.

But when pressed in 1977, she asserted: 'Cousins has great potential, particularly if he stays as dedicated to the sport as he is now. His free skating has made a great impression with the international judges. He is an exceptionally good spinner. His spins are fast and very well-centred. His jumps are high, sure and strong – performed with a lot of abandon. He has very good stamina, giving the impression of being as strong at the finish as at the beginning of his five minutes.'

Like most outstanding jumpers, Cousins has been fearless on the ice, taking calculated risks and accepting injuries as an occupational hazard. During the winter of 1977, he turned up at a skaters' ball with one hand protected to nurse a slight sprain.

Only after persistent enquiries did he confess: 'I did it landing a triple axel.' At that time, the first triple axel jump had yet to be achieved in a championship.

John Curry's keen legion of fans could never conceive that anyone else would ever match their idol's controlled and contrived ability to fit so well into every bar of music.

But Cousins has shrewdly used his music to help create an abandoned, dashing, younger image and a more robust, daring athleticism which excites and appeals even more to many connoisseurs as well as to the public at large.

His musical preference weighs heavily in favour of Stanley Black. 'Black's arrangements suit my skating well,' says Robin, 'because there is so much dramatic scope for timing my highlights.' He listens avidly to music, always

Co-authors in harmony – Robin Cousins and Howard Bass

with ears alerted for skating suitability, and helped sometimes by brother Nick, who has played bassoon for the Bristol Symphony Orchestra.

When coached for three seasons (until 1976) by Gladys Hogg at Queen's Ice Skating Club, London, Robin had to rise at 6 a.m. to make sure of precious ice space before crowded public sessions began. How else could he have perfected those five Innsbruck Olympic triples – toe loop, salchow (combined with a double loop), loop, another toe loop (linked to a double flip) and the final spectacular salchow?

The need for more practice time and space inspired his move to Denver, thanks to benevolent training sponsorship from a Scottish building company which sought no publicity in return.

With a slender frame just touching 6 ft, Cousins is the envy of many skaters with weight problems. 'I can eat exactly what I like – and do,' he grins. His only

13

frugal meal has been breakfast, just corn flakes and toast before training.

The social sacrifices are considerable in a top skater's early to bed, early-to-rise schedule. Utter dedication is essential if the highest possible pinnacle is to be reached.

After Innsbruck in 1976, in his disarmingly quiet and gentle off-ice manner, Robin told me: 'I mean to go on until 1980 and hope I shall then be able to retain the Olympic title for Britain at Lake Placid.' With mind thus resolved, he became a determined, irresistible force that nothing and nobody could stop.

What follows is his factually honest autobiography, the frank, unadorned story of a still-young man's fascinating career. It is in no sense 'ghosted'. Following this page, all the words printed in large type are Robin's own, spoken into a tape-recorder and simply edited by me without expansion.

But because Robin is so modest and unassuming, more needed to be told. Facts he would never relate in self-praise, with my relevant comments to supplement his own, are added in a smaller, distinctive style of type.

Acknowledgment is made for retrospective extracts from some of my championship reports and observations originally appearing in the *Daily Telegraph* and *Sunday Telegraph* in London and also in *Skating*, the official journal of the United States Figure Skating Association.

One hopes the whole presents a fair picture of how a very determined boy overcame many difficulties and setbacks to attain a most laudable goal, and, while doing so, in his own way promoted international goodwill.

Howard Bass

1
A Dream Comes True

With the most important moment of his sporting career only days away, Robin Cousins looked impressive during his final work-outs on each of the three ice rinks used at Lake Placid during practice for the 1980 Olympic figure skating.

It was a long time since he had looked so fit and confident, obviously enjoying every moment of his training under the watchful eyes of his mentors, Carlo and Christa Fassi.

The landings of his jumps on exactly the right part of the blade were so precisely timed that each giant leap was made to look much simpler than it really was.

After the opening ceremony of the Games, however, Cousins lost an hour's important practice-time when he was caught in the inevitable traffic jam on the way back to the village. The journey took two hours and he did not have time to get into town for his free skating practice.

It was not only on the ice that Cousins made an impression. When the British Olympic Association organized a special press conference to satisfy a swelling demand from media personnel, the tall West Countryman sat easily on the concert platform in the same plush armchair used by Lord Killanin for his International Olympic Committee policy statements.

Remarkably cool, composed and articulate, the European Champion dealt with every question patiently and succinctly. Asked why he left England, Cousins calmly retorted: 'I have not left England. Bristol is still my home and I still represent my local club.

'I train in America simply because of the facilities offered. In the States, most rinks are for club participants, with ample ice time for championship preparations. In Britain, public sessions – as distinct from club activities – dominate the ice time. In Denver, where I train, there are seven rinks. In London there are only two, and neither of them are Olympic-size.'

Asked how well he knew Charlie Tickner, the American then widely considered the main danger to his gold medal aspirations, Cousins said: 'We live only five blocks apart, but hardly see each other during training. We have been close rivals and good friends, too, for several years now.'

Did he regard Tickner as the man to beat? 'I have learned not to regard any one person like that,' he replied. 'There are any of half a dozen in this event who could produce the right form at the right time to win. I just hope it may be me.'

Did he owe everything to Fassi? 'No, I select my own music, do my own choreography, plan my own programme and decide what to include. But a diamond cannot become a diamond on its own. It has to be cut by someone else.'

The 8500 capacity crowd at the final free skating would be likely to spur him on. 'I thrive on audience reaction,' he emphasized.

When the Olympic contest began in earnest, Cousins made a fairly satisfactory start in the compulsory figures, ending a handily-placed fourth behind Jan Hoffmann, the East German leader, Charlie Tickner, the hope of the host nation, and David Santee, the American number two.

Although Vladimir Kovalev, the Russian World Champion, was passed fit to start, he later withdrew. Kovalev had not been well for a week and had seldom attended practice sessions.

The first figure, the rocker, showed Hoffmann, Tickner and Cousins to be clearly the dominant trio. The Bristolian put down a good tracing and three judges had him above Tickner.

Before he went on the ice for his third figure, the paragraph bracket, Cousins was told that a son had been born to his brother Martin's wife, June, in Roehampton. The news had a tonic effect on him, his parents and his other brother, Nick, all watching anxiously at the rinkside.

Hoffmann maintained his lead in both the second figure and the third, the paragraph loop. Tickner had greater difficulty in staying above Cousins and, when all three figures were over, it appeared likely that the three would go on to share the medals, despite Santee's late spurt with a particularly good final figure.

Cousins rose from fourth to second after a brilliant performance in the short free programme, narrowing the margin separating him from Hoffmann. The new order of the four front-runners now read: Hoffmann, Cousins, Tickner and Santee.

Drawn thirteenth in the order of skating, a number which had been previously lucky for Cousins, the tall Englishman looked supremely assured and his rivals appeared to feel the pressure much more. Hoffmann and Tickner, who skated after Cousins, lost precious ground – each marked lower than Cousins across the board.

Accomplishing with ease an optional triple cherry following the obligatory double loop – the jump combination he had chosen not to attempt a month previously in Gothenburg – Cousins gave a flawless demonstration of the seven elements required in his two-minute performance.

Comfortably winning this section of the competition, he gained a maximum six mark from the Canadian judge for artistic presentation. Seven of the other eight judges awarded 5·9 and three also gave him 5·9 for technical merit.

Hoffmann made no error but jumped the same two jumps as Cousins in reverse order – less difficult and therefore worth fewer marks. His presentation was also marked appreciably lower. Tickner spoiled his combination, failing to land the double loop correctly after a triple cherry.

Santee produced his personal best, excelling with a well-landed triple cherry and

Happy days in a daze on a dais – the 1980 Lake Placid Olympic medallists, with Champion Cousins flanked by runner-up Jan Hoffmann (right) and third-placed Charlie Tickner

a confident flying jump-camel spin. Despite this, like his compatriot Tickner, he was overtaken by Cousins. So the stage looked set for a thrilling duel between Cousins and Hoffmann in the final free skating.

While every Cousins fan in Lake Placid went around with butterflies in the stomach during the countdown hours of the final day, the man who had the right to be far more tense looked the calmest and coolest of all.

A little after midday, he glided on to the ice for his final fifty minutes' practice, just seven hours before the Olympic men's free skating was due to begin. While Carlo and Christa Fassi watched hawk-eyed from the rink barrier, he went through the highlights of his programme stage by stage, jumping and spinning immaculately as if it were the contest itself.

Some thought he would elect to walk through the session and be satisfied merely to loosen up the limbs and feel his blades edging along the ice. But he chose instead to attempt everything, only hours before the most vital five minutes of his career.

His confidence and timing, his easy chatting and laughing with his coaches, seemed wholly incongruous to his nervous supporters, who followed his every move with bated breath. Most would have settled then for just seeing him come off the ice free of injury. Surely that was the uppermost thought in the minds of his parents. The session mercifully over, they joined him for lunch — a light meal, yet rich in protein and ending with his favourite pancake, for Cousins has never needed to be a weight-watcher.

At last the big moment came and, that evening, an inspired Robin won the Olympic gold medal by a whisker. Hoffmann lost by a slender overall margin, but there was no doubt that the right man had won, a fact which Hoffmann and third-placed Charlie Tickner sportingly acknowledged.

The East German had begun his free skating with a distinct points advantage from the figures. Cousins whittled that away and could still afford a mistake and win — that was the measure of his world superiority in free skating.

The first of the four leaders to skate, Cousins mesmerized the crowd with a spell-binding succession of difficult manoeuvres, all interlinked and presented so smoothly and artistically that, to the layman, it looked too easy.

That is the mark of a master in any sport. He revolutionized conceptions of free skating, based on a growing acceptance that mighty leaps are not the be-all-and-end-all. He deliberately did not overload his programme with triples, but emphasized versatility and all-round competence in every department, not least the spins, the true art of which he not only resurrected but greatly advanced.

Cousins succeeded that day with three great triples, two cherries and a salchow, but two-footed a triple loop — almost certainly the reason he gained no six, for the rest was sheer perfection. Even so, eight of the nine judges saw fit to award 5·9 for presentation and three of them gave the same high mark for technical merit.

In humorous spirit at a press conference during the 1980 Lake Placid Olympics

Hoffmann had probably never skated better. Mindful that it was to be his last season, he threw himself into it, with everything to gain and nothing to lose. He included five triples — lutz, loop, salchow and two cherries. After Hoffmann had skated and been assessed overall as second best, albeit narrowly, the only possible contender to deny Cousins the title could have been Tickner, who skated last.

But the 1978 World Champion was too tense and made enough errors for the outcome to become quickly apparent. Six of the nine judges at the end had Cousins clearly ahead despite his one error, despite Hoffmann's lead in the figures and despite the East German gaining fractionally more points.

Cousins's victory at Lake Placid was a great fillip to the sport, particularly in Britain, where it stimulated a much increased call on ice rinks already bursting at the seams. One hopes that, in consequence, public authorities and private enterprise alike will be inspired to invest in the extra arenas needed if worthy national successors are to be produced. Until ice becomes more plentiful for skating, obviously the highest standards will be more difficult to achieve.

I spent only a week at Denver between the 1980 European Championships and the Olympics, but looked forward to the day that we were able to leave for Lake Placid. Interest was beginning to fade regarding my European title win and now centred on my training in the United States and being about to compete in America against the Americans.

Some of the local newspapers and television people were very interested in the story that Charlie Tickner and I were both training and living in the same city and were probably going to be two of the biggest rivals at the Games.

I was therefore quite happy to get away from Denver to begin final preparations at Lake Placid, although the length of time I spent there before the competition began — almost two weeks — was perhaps a little too long. You had to try to maintain your psychological momentum, but it was the same for everybody and we just about managed to cope with that.

But the night before we left Denver — *we* being Carlo and Christa Fassi and their family, national champions Emi Watanabe of Japan, Kristi Wegelius of Finland, Karena Richardson and myself — there was a going-away party given by the Wylies, with whom I lived, and their friends, the family of Dr Hugh Graham.

Paul and Brenda Wylie had made banners which they had hung in the rink and there was a tremendous send-off. It was very personal and I really appreciated all the training days that we had had prior to the Olympics. It was a big deal for all of us and rewarding that we were able to get together and show our appreciation to each other for all the help that had gone into our preparations.

This happy send-off continued as far as Denver airport, where we popped a bottle of champagne and were able to drink an appropriate toast. So we all left in good spirits, or vice-versa, very much ready and eager.

Everything in the Olympic athletes' village seemed fine. The bedrooms were very small, but if you only used them for sleeping it was not too bad. The recreation facilities, the food, theatre and cinema were all excellent. There was a great atmosphere.

All the athletes were having a good time, playing each other at pinball, watching the various entertainments together and just generally enjoying each other's company without thinking of anything else that was going on in the world at the time.

It was unfortunate that Lake Placid was caught up in the turmoil of international politics – not just concerning Afghanistan, but other issues that people were dragging into the Olympics just for publicity – and it was nice to know that nobody inside the village cared about this.

All the participants were concerned about was having a good time, performing well and maybe picking up some medals. The friendly relationships were really heartening. Because many of us had two weeks for training, but for only three hours on the ice each day, we were happy for the extra recreational amenities available. Otherwise, I think we would have become bored and very nervous quite quickly.

The men drew the same figures for the Olympics as we had at the European Championships, although they were on the other foot. We drew left foot here and right foot in Gothenburg.

I had just finished my second figure when a telephone message from England brought news that my sister-in-law, June, Martin's wife, had given birth to a son. So my nephew, Robin Clifford, arrived in the world on the same day that I skated my first section of the Olympic competition.

My figures were below the standard I had achieved in Gothenburg, but I was pleased with my fourth place and believe the top four or five all produced tracings of a high calibre.

It must have been difficult to choose between us. I know we all gave the judges some tough times through the competition and it was very gratifying to hear some of them say that the figures laid down at this Championship were some of the best that they had seen in recent years.

We – that is the Fassis and I – were not unduly worried about the position at the end of the figures. We had hoped for maybe third or fourth or even fifth place. So, in fourth position and within striking distance of third or even second, I knew I was in with a chance. I knew, too, that I would have my work cut out, but that is the way I like it.

It would have been more comfortable, of course, to have been as near to the leader as I was in Gothenburg, but I wasn't bothered overmuch. I had always made it hard for myself in the past. That is not something that I purposefully made a habit of, but I was quite content to be where I was and was drawn well in the order for the short programme – second after David Santee in the last group.

The short programme training had been going a lot better here than in Gothenburg and I was very pleased with my progress. At practice in the morning, I felt very excited and maybe a little too eager. Jumps were keeling over in the air – no real mistakes, but just a little bit off. Christa and I were not worried and Carlo was happy to let things ride through; I believe the three of us felt fairly confident that I could get things right in the competition proper.

When it began that afternoon, I had my first taste of how much Americans in the audience (as well as my own British supporters) were behind me. The Americans, I know, had seen a lot of me in the past year on television and I was aware that I had featured in a spate of news coverage, but I was not prepared for quite the amount of support they gave me.

The number of telegrams I received from all over America, from many people that I did not know, as well as from Europe and home especially, was unbelievable and a tremendous boost. Perhaps in consequence, the short programme I did was one of the best and cleanest performances I had ever accomplished and some onlookers were kind enough to suggest that it was the best example of a short programme that one could wish to see.

I was very confident with the jumps. They were very solid and the spins were as good as I think they could have been. As for the presentation, one of the judges thought it was up to the perfect six and the others thought it was worth 5·9, so I was naturally very pleased and it much improved my position before the long programme.

It was a real thrill, but I knew that if I was going to equal that kind of performance in the long programme, I had a lot of work to do. I had put great pressure on myself and felt I had set a level difficult to maintain, but one that people would expect of me.

I do not know that I really thought I would win. Hoffmann still had a very definite lead accruing from the figures. There was no doubt about that. He still had nine first places going into the long programme and, compared with the corresponding stage in the European Championships, I was not so close.

But Carlo still insisted that it was close enough for me to win and, as I walked around the village, people kept coming up and saying 'yes, you've got it, no problem.'

I suddenly realized how many people already had the gold medal hanging round my neck, yet I still had ahead of me the hardest task of all.

Some people ask me if, in circumstances like that, I could sleep well the night before. It did not worry me the night before, but the morning was a little different. Nevertheless, the training went very well at the final practice and Carlo

With parents Fred and Jo during a break in the 1980 Lake Placid Olympics

said: 'I just hope you don't leave this all behind at the training and come out and blow it tonight.'

I felt I would be able to do us justice if the kind of support already shown was maintained. The support was in fact about three times greater. It was just incredible. There were banners up all over the place, from Americans and Brits alike; the Union Jacks were flying and it was tremendous.

Although Carlo was not too happy with my order, which was first of the final six, I was personally quite content to skate first and leave everybody else to follow. I preferred it that way.

As it happened, Charlie did not enjoy waiting around and hearing all the thunderous ovations, and if it had been me, maybe it would have affected my performance – kicking my heels and listening to everyone else's marks and applause. No, I certainly do not think it would have helped me at all to have had to skate after three Americans in America, regardless of what the judges decided to do.

When I went on the ice for those all-important five minutes, I felt very confident and was lifted throughout by the wonderful support of the audience. The only slight error obviously was my landing on the triple loop and it really was an unnecessary slip. It was not a mistake as such; just one of those things that happen at the time. I knew as soon as that lapse was over. I took a glance over at Carlo, who had taken a couple of steps back away from the rink barrier, and I thought, 'OK, that's done now. You can't do anything about it. Just do the rest properly.'

I did not panic. I just went on as if I had landed that jump perfectly – and the rest of the programme came out for me better than it had in Gothenburg. The judges rewarded me with very high marks and I was overwhelmed at the reaction of the crowd.

Having seen the way things had gone in the short programme, I think many Americans had decided that there probably was not going to be a United States victory – so, in their view, the next best thing was for me to win rather than Hoffmann. The switchover of support was quite amazing.

I picked up so many flowers and little presents from the ice that, by the time I had left the rink and put on my skate-guards, a TV interviewer pulled me away to ask what I thought about my performance. By the time that chat was over, Hoffmann's marks were about to be read and I listened attentively. Experts took them down and were trying to work out comparisons, and I said at the time that I didn't think I had won.

With that, I walked from the adjacent training rink where we had done the interview back into the competitors' area. I was waiting to get an orange squash when I saw Christa, who walked towards me with a very blank look on her face and I thought, 'Oh well, that's it. She has seen the scores and Hoffmann is still above me.'

Instead, she looked straight at me and said: 'Well, you are there, but Charlie has to skate yet,' and she continued to walk on past me. I was stunned because this meant I had pulled above Hoffmann.

My mother looked worse than I felt, which must have been just awful, because I sat down for a while and could not watch any of the remaining four skaters. The waiting around at this point was worse than the waiting around before the actual performance. I think I could have gone into the training rink and skated over my programme several times and still have felt better than just having to wait.

At this stage, I did not know whether Charlie needed to skate well or otherwise for me to win. The crucial thing was what was going to happen to his placements (ordinals) in relation to Jan and myself, that could make the difference.

I could not bear to sit around any more and walked back into the training rink to watch Linda Fratianne practising. I was sitting there when a couple walked across from the main arena. Linda came over to me and asked: 'How

Robin acknowledges the tribute of his fans outside his home, before a civic reception given by the Mayor of Bristol in March, 1980

How Bristol's citizens paid tribute to their idol as Robin approached Bristol City Council House

did Charlie do?' and I said: 'He hasn't finished yet.'

With that, one of the newly-arrived couples called out: 'Oh, yes he has and his marks are already out.' So I walked back to the arena and someone shouted: 'Congratulations, you've made it.'

My mother and father were standing there. I ran up to them and suddenly Carlo, Christa and everybody seemed to be all over me. I never really did know how Tickner skated, but apparently the ordinals did not change and I ended up with a 6–3 victory over Hoffmann.

Everything went a sort of blank from then until I found myself standing ready to go out to the awards. By now I think the whole audience had guessed the result from the scores relayed on TV monitor screens: such news travels fast even though no announcement had been made.

I never did understand the lady who was trying to tell me what I was supposed to do when going out for the ceremony. Standing there, waiting to go on to the ice, with camera bulbs flashing all around, people screaming congratulations from all sides and flowers dropping on our heads – it was really quite something.

When the fanfare was sounding and the three of us went up to stand beside our respective places, there was one step on to each podium, or so I thought. But mine being the highest, there were one-and-a-half steps, and when they made the announcement that I was Olympic Champion there was no way my feet wanted to take me *anywhere*, let alone up one-and-a-half steps.

They seemed stuck to the ice and when I tried to get up on that podium, I literally tripped up it. But I made it up there and the ovation was unbelievable; it was like being in London.

The raising of the Union Jack was an almost indescribable moment – something that you can visualize and marvel at on TV, but it is not easy for me to explain how I felt at the time.

It was great that the Union Jack was between myself and my parents. They were looking at one side of it, I was looking at the other. So, as it was slowly going up, I lost sight of them for a while. But when the Union Jack was finally above our heads, we were looking directly at each other. So I was able to know how they were feeling and they could see how I was feeling, but it is difficult to describe that to anyone else.

The national anthem was being played at the same time and my only 'complaint' is that *God Save The Queen* does not last long enough for the flag to get to the top. This was the second time I had won an international championship and on each occasion our national anthem had finished before they had hoisted the flag. When someone from another nation wins, the national anthem seems to last ten minutes longer, so I think two verses of ours should be played.

This huge gold medal around my neck was just unbelievable; I had to give it back immediately after leaving the ice for it to be engraved, so I lost it for a day!

After the ceremony, I began to lose track of who I talked to or what I was talking about. But I knew I had won the gold medal and my mother was in tears.

I saw Maggie Fell with some of her friends who had travelled all the way from Scotland. There were bouquets from local kids I had trained with in Placid when I was there for summer seminars.

America has produced some great world champions who were in Lake Placid at the time, people like Dorothy Hamill, Peggy Fleming, Dick Button, Tenley Albright, Carol Heiss and Hayes Jenkins. They and so many others prominent at national level were all gathered around the action in the arena.

The support and help and friendly comments that I have had from such people, not just in Lake Placid but throughout my career, have been quite astonishing and I shall be eternally grateful for all the assistance they have given me. I have always been concerned that my achievements would justify so much kind interest.

'First Cousins – Great Britain.'

Those momentous words, as I stood on the Olympic winner's podium at Lake Placid, followed by the emotion-tugging strains of *God Save The Queen* and the ceremonial raising of the Union Jack, symbolized the goal I had set my heart on and striven towards through years of dedicated training and social sacrifices.

That climactic moment of glory as the treasured Olympic gold medal was placed around my neck ended an era that I knew had been worthwhile, bringing much pleasure along the way and, at the same time, preparing me for a professional career doing what I most enjoyed.

Yet, I cannot help but reflect, my whole life could have been entirely different without the curious hand played by Fate fourteen years earlier.

2
Handstands & Cartwheels

My father had been a footballer – he played in goal for Millwall – and was more or less expecting his three sons to be footballers, too. The earliest involvement in sport that I can remember was when I was four or five and my Dad used to kick a ball around with my two older brothers.

Much to my Dad's dismay, no matter how hard he tried to bring me into their games, I did not want to kick the ball and would much rather be doing handstands and cartwheels and even did them when my arm was in a sling after a childhood accident. Sitting in the garden, I had chopped the top of my finger off in the act of trying to fold a deckchair.

So, after watching my junior one-armed gymnastics, my father, very bewildered, finally said: 'Well, forget this' (meaning the football) and, very shortly afterwards, I started dancing classes at the local Joan Watson School of Dancing in Sea Mills, Bristol.

This I enjoyed, though the training was hard. I used to stand behind the settee and do my exercises every night. My Mum would have to sit there and make me do them properly, as on my own I just did the nice bits where you run around the floor, leap into the air and fall flat on your back. But I persevered and progressed to the third grade. I also came away with honours in my ballet exams before the day arrived which was to influence the whole course of my life.

It was a very hot summer's day in 1965 at Bournemouth, where my parents, brothers and myself were on holiday. Everyone appeared to be out on the beach sunbathing and there seemed hardly any room left there for us. My brothers decided they wanted to go and play mini-golf, so my father took them. I was too young for that, so I was told, and was carted off into town with my Mum, who, clad in shorts and a T-shirt, was looking for somewhere nice to cool off.

Staring at us invitingly was the ice rink, so we decided to go and see what was happening there. In we trotted and, within twenty minutes, I was standing on the ice with my little skates on, doddering around. My mother, looking for somebody to help me, suddenly found herself at the instruction desk paying for me to have a lesson.

The professional, after the lesson, asked my mother where I did my skating and she informed him that this was my first time on ice. Until we told him we were from Bristol, where there was no rink, he didn't really believe that I hadn't had skates on before. Then he told us that an ice rink was being built in Bristol.

Back home after that, every other Saturday, when we went to get my hair cut we had to go and see how the new rink-building was progressing. But it was not until nearly a year after the new Silver Blades rink had opened that I started in the children's courses under George Rose.

I attended my first children's 'learn to skate' class and, once I knew I could get from the barrier on one side of the rink to the other, I was trying to do the same things as other children who were having their ninth or tenth class, while I was still only on my second.

At the end of the course, the teacher wrote on my report card: 'This boy will never be a skater. He wants to do everything at once.'

I was always being told off – for doing what I shouldn't be doing and for attempting what other people were doing. Even so, out of the children's classes came the chance of a Christmas present. What did I want? I wanted some skating lessons.

So we decided to look at the instruction board. I could have so many lessons with this professional or so many with that professional – one being more expensive than the other. 'Oh, I want to have lessons with her,' I said, looking at Pam Davies. She had smiled at me that morning. It was the beginning of a seven-and-a-half-year relationship with Pam and the beginning of my real skating career.

My private lessons with Pam began on a once-a-week basis each Saturday morning, and then, gradually, as I progressed and entered competitions at my local Bristol rink, we upped the lessons to two or three a week, the extra ones in mid-week afternoons after school.

Both my brothers at the time were playing rugby for the school and Nick was playing in the school orchestra, so Mum found herself frequently coming to the ice rink in the morning, going to the rugby in the afternoon and to a concert at night – to see all three of us doing what made us tick.

Pam was a great teacher and I look back on those formative years as some of the best so far as enjoyment was concerned. I cannot really believe that I would have done as well as I am doing now if I had not started off with Pam.

She was always emphasizing that it is one thing simply being able to do something technically well, but quite another doing it with style. We would spend hours working on the lesser jumps when I knew I wanted to try the harder things that the other kids were doing – but, until I could accomplish the lesser jumps and spins properly, she would not let me do anything more advanced.

Looking back now, it is obvious that Pam's methods were the best help I

Above left Dad holds on to me at the seaside, with brothers Nick and Martin
Above right As a little boy, I preferred doing handstands and cartwheels when my brothers kicked a ball about
Opposite right Cricket was not my forte, but at least I dressed for the part!
Opposite far right With Nick and Martin again – all dressed up and nowhere to go
Below opposite Enriching the quality of the church choir at St Edyth's, Sea Mills, Bristol

could have had at the time, because I have won events since purely because what I did was done well, and I never attempted too much too early.

When I began to take lessons with Pam, I had never skated competitively. By the time I left her seven or eight years later, I was already number three in my country, and had won over twenty junior events, including the British novice and British junior titles. Yes, I am very happy to say that everything I did in those first seven or eight years, including competing in a European Championship and a World Championship, was all due to Pam and the hard work that she put in with me.

When I was a novice, school was never a difficulty. School always came first. My skating was done in the late afternoons and evenings and most of my competitions took place at weekends. But, as I gradually progressed through the junior events, travelling to places like Billingham, Birmingham and Nottingham, I began to find it necessary to ask for a day off from school in order to compete – and, when you are eleven or twelve, this is hardly ideal so far as education is concerned, and the teachers were not too enthusiastic.

When I started to bring my trophies to school, it seemed to make a difference and I think they realized that, after all, my requests for time off were justifiable and that I was not skating entirely for fun and merely in order to get out of school.

I was excused from my Friday afternoon games lessons at the Sea Mills junior school for an extra hour's training. When I moved into the senior school at Henbury Comprehensive, I was given the best treatment possible with regard to my skating, freed from the less necessary periods at school in order to stay on at the ice rink some mornings and again to forego games lessons for afternoon skating.

My headmaster was very co-operative, giving all the encouragement I needed for competitions, but embarrassing me somewhat when successful. Whenever I won, somehow he would find out and announce it over the school intercom, so the cheers from some kids were mingled with jeers from others. At school you naturally get jealousy, and it is hard to overcome. But having done so, the other kids realized skating wasn't a silly sport and they didn't mind that I made a name for myself around the country as a junior competitor.

I was still at senior school when I was entered for my first senior British Championship, just before Christmas 1972. Then, when I was qualifying internationally, my headmaster had to be approached because the time when I should be competing in the European Championships in Cologne was also the time when I should have been sitting for exams at school.

So we had to decide what I should do. It was the final year, when one was (then) allowed to leave school at fifteen and not sixteen, and, as my headmaster was reasonably happy with the reports that I had had, he more or less said that, if I was intending to take up a career in skating, the best thing I could do was to go to the championships and leave school at the Easter which followed.

This I did and, without my schools' understanding help, I would have found training and competing much more difficult; looking back, I am grateful for all concerned in both schools for their co-operation. Nothing could have been better than doing what I most enjoyed and knowing at the same time that it was

Relaxing at home, after my operation, doing what I enjoy – drawing

not done behind people's backs, and especially those of the school and education board.

It was decided that I would go to a comprehensive school, mainly so that I could more easily continue my skating training. Both my brothers were at Bristol Grammar School and each was good at academic work as well as sport, particularly cricket and rugby.

Nick was also an excellent musician and was constantly called on to play his bassoon in local orchestras. My father would go with my brothers to rugby and soccer and the whole family would go to listen to Nick playing in concerts. So we were all constantly preoccupied with our activities.

Both my parents were remarkably adept at dividing themselves into three or more 'pieces' to pay equal attention to all of us in our early stages. I think this is one of the reasons why we have all managed to stay so close and help each other so much – even now, when we are a lot older and well advanced in our chosen careers.

After nearly a year of training, I suddenly discovered that Pam had decided it was about time I took my first National Skating Association proficiency tests. By this time, not only was I working with her on free skating and figures, but also on ice dancing. So, in fact, I took my first three tests – preliminary ice dance, preliminary ice figure and bronze free – all on the same day – and passed each at the first attempt.

This justified my working for higher standard tests, entering local competitions and later travelling to Brighton, Bournemouth, Southampton and Birmingham, where I finished among the top three in practically every junior competition.

In 1969 at Billingham, I won my first national title, the British Novice Championship – now called the British Primary Championship – and in 1972 went back to Billingham to win the Junior Championship of Great Britain. This entitled me to compete in the National Senior Championship at Richmond in December the same year.

Things were now moving swiftly. I knew that a reasonably good performance in the British Seniors might even earn selection for an international championship début the same season. Perhaps others foresaw this possibility, because, in the meantime, I had an invitation from my National Association to compete in the Grand Prix at St Gervais, France.

This is a kind of B-grade international event, to which nations send their up-and-coming skaters to get a taste of international atmosphere before embarking on the big circuit. So it was that I arrived in St Gervais to meet a young American who was likewise appearing in *his* first international – Charlie Tickner. This was to be the first of many meetings. Charlie went on to win the event and I was placed only seventh.

The 1972 junior title win was the start of a long line of competitions in which

I relied on my free skating to pull me up from my figures position. In fact, I was fourth out of four at the Billingham Junior Championship and then won the free skating section to pull up to first. Then, in St Gervais, I was fourteenth in figures out of eighteen skaters, then finished fourth and fifth in the two free skating sections to end overall seventh. So here I was at the beginning of a 'let's work on the figures' routine.

Prior to this very full 1972–73 season, I had started to go to London once a week to take lessons from the famous Gladys Hogg, MBE, at Queen's Ice Club, to get experience in competitions and training of a kind that Pam had not been able to provide because she had not been a championship competitor herself.

Working with these two professionals was a big advantage – one being youthful and bright with new ideas and the other with a wealth of experience behind her – which together helped me enormously.

'For services to skating' was the citation when Gladys Hogg was awarded the Medal of the British Empire by the Queen in 1969. Her instructional colleague, Erik Van der Weyden, has written: 'It is no exaggeration to assert that Gladys Hogg lives for the rink and on it. She has made the rink her habitat.

'It would be incorrect to describe it as an obsession. It is more than that; it is an all-absorbing enthusiasm for what constitutes her career; she is forever striving to attain still greater efficiency.'

Possessor of five national gold test medals, the versatile Gladys as a girl gained three national roller dance victories, partnered by John Blaver, before winning three British open professional titles, for ice dancing and pair skating with Ronnie Baker in 1947 and again for ice dancing with Bernard Spencer in 1949.

World Champions in her roll of distinguished pupils are John and Jennifer Nicks, Lawrence Demmy with Jean Westwood, Courtney Jones with June Markham and with Doreen Denny, and Bernard Ford with Diane Towler.

The encouragement of individuality and creative thought on the part of the pupil is an integral feature of Miss Hogg's tuitional technique. 'Free skating,' she emphasizes, 'is designed to bring out each skater's own personality, to give full scope to express oneself.' The galaxy of star talent she has nurtured is significant testimony to her success.

Gladys Hogg is a great character, always endeavouring to make you work and try new things, and her vast experience from many competitions and from training many leading performers showed quite clearly during my first international season. I was able to benefit from her experience just by listening to her and working with her for three years.

She took my compulsory figures to pieces, more or less, and managed to drill them into championship standard. Gladys spent much time teaching me the senior figures and I was able to use Pam's style and lines, making them look good as well as knowing they were technically correct. The combination of the two seemed to put me on the right lines to work when I went to Carlo Fassi. After that, I just had to brush up what I had already learned and get it all consistent to start winning.

3
Delayed World Début

26 April 1972, marked the beginning of ten months' unusually rapid progress so early in a championship competitor's career. That day at Billingham, although fourth in the figures, Cousins overhauled three rivals in the free to win the British junior title. It qualified him to compete in the National Senior Championships at Richmond the following December, when his form in third place prompted selection with John Curry and Michael Fish to contest the European Championships two months later. Being thrown in at the deep end so soon could have unnerved some, but the early experience in top company proved invaluable to Robin Cousins and showed he had a good 'big match' temperament.

Selected for his international début after only two months in senior ranks, schoolboy Cousins must have felt awe-struck in the European Championships at Cologne Ice Stadium in February, 1973, but he never showed it. Fifteenth overall and fourteenth in the free was an encouraging start in a pretty successful meeting for some of his team-mates. Jean Scott won the women's silver medal, Glyn Watts and Hilary Green took the bronze for ice dancing and John Curry, fourth in the men's, narrowly missed increasing the national medal haul.

The 1972 British Senior Championships provided my first confrontation with John Curry, who was defending his title against Michael Fish, a young northern skater, and myself. I was third out of the three of us in the figures – no surprises there – but did manage to come second in both the short and long programmes, though I still finished third overall.

The sequel was a rather unexpected invitation from the National Skating Association to represent Great Britain at the European Championships in Cologne, West Germany. Thus I was about to embark seriously on an international career and, after more than seven years under the guidance of Pam Davies, it was decided that it would be better for me to be trained by Gladys Hogg in London on a more exclusive basis.

I hated leaving Pam, but we both realized that I did then need to be guided properly on the international circuit and this was something that Pam was unable to do so well as Gladys. So I made the switch and started to train at Queen's Ice Club just prior to Cologne.

I was quite overawed on arrival in Cologne, meeting up with so many established stars whom I had only seen on television, having stayed up late at night to watch them in previous seasons.

There were twenty-two competitors and my overall finishing place of fifteenth – including fourteenth in the short free and thirteenth in the final free – was far better than I had dared to expect. Again, a relatively low figure placing, but I was not last, and therefore quite happy.

The first transatlantic assignment for Cousins was to represent Britain in the new annual Skate Canada international competitions in October, 1973, in Calgary, Alberta. The series replaced the North American Championships, which had been restricted to United States and Canadian competitors, and this highly successful initial meeting took place at the Stampede Corral Stadium, named after the city's celebrated rodeo shows.

Cousins, who had left school the preceding Easter, came eleventh in the figures among opponents with far greater international experience. It was just the kind of outing to hasten the progress of a fine young prospect. In the short free, he moved up a place, due largely to an impressive double axel. Finally tenth overall, he finished fifth in the free skating and the Canadian winner, Toller Cranston, was sufficiently impressed to say at the time that he believed 'this British youngster has the makings of a future world champion.'

It was a successful outing for the British, with a gold medal for Glyn Watts and Hilary Green in the ice dance event and a bronze for Jean Scott in the women's. The team's joyous journey home was on Jean's twenty-first birthday and the Air Canada flight captain turned up trumps by providing a special cake and champagne to complete their happiness.

Having survived a reasonably successful European début, it was up to me to take my next proficiency test – the inter-gold figures – in order to stay on in senior ranks. In 1972, I had been eligible for the British Senior Championships as a privilege accorded to the reigning junior champion, the only skater able to qualify without needing to pass the inter-gold (a national rule since changed so that, now, having once competed at senior level, one may continue to do so regardless of tests passed).

I managed to pass the inter-gold during the summer of 1973 and, in the autumn, found myself on my first trip to Canada to compete in Skate Canada in Calgary, Alberta. It was the first event of its kind in North America, having just been reorganized in a new annual format, virtually replacing the previous biennial North American Championships.

It was a very good competition and a great experience which I enjoyed immensely, finishing tenth out of twelve. I had gone there as a nobody and came away as a nobody, but had gained plenty from watching everyone else – learning how others compete and how they withstand the pressures – and I knew that next time I went abroad to compete, I should be able to put to good use my experience in Calgary, in addition to what I had learned in Cologne.

Back to Richmond and the British Championships of December, 1973, when I was to be runner-up to John Curry for the first time. John was way ahead in both the figures and the free skating, but I was quite content to be a pretty good second and to prove that much more worthy of selection, not only for the European Championships of 1974 in Zagreb, Yugoslavia, but also for the World Championships in Munich.

The Zagreb European event produced mixed fortunes. I was placed higher in the previous season but then experienced an upset. At the end of the short programme practice, I had a very nasty fall and appeared to have twisted my ankle. So, here I was in only my second international season and, already, things had started to go wrong.

Cousins made his second appearance in the European Championships at the Sports Hall, Zagreb, in January, 1974. Suffering heavy bruises on crashing from a triple salchow jump during practice he was only sixteenth in the figures but everyone knew he would climb higher. Fourteenth after the short free, he later moved up to eleventh overall and a creditable sixth in the free, landing a clean triple salchow although wincing from what was thought to be a sprained ankle. At sixteen years of age, he already looked a tremendous prospect.

Alas, the injury proved to be a chipped ankle bone, not diagnosed until after Robin was forced to withdraw from what would have been his world championship début that March in Munich.

We consulted a doctor, who was later to be consulted many more times – Dr Wolf-Dieter Montag, who was the West German team physician. The British never had and probably never will have, their own team doctor at championships and so we are forced to rely on other countries in this respect. Luckily for the British team, Dr Montag seemed always available.

I managed to skate the short programme and even pull up one or two places but, the following day, I had great difficulty even standing on my ankle, let alone putting on any skates. We got the doctor to strap it but I was unable to practise. The International Skating Union was approached and permission gained to have a separate practice of my own, when the doctor would strap my ankle and strap me into my skating boot. Because of this difficult ritual, my boot would stay on until the time I competed and this happened a good two hours before the competition.

The perks of getting well-known – meeting Miss World of 1972 (Belinda Green of Australia)

In the warm-up, I had to get on to the ice and skate round and round in circles until I could break through the pain barrier. Somehow I got through the event and even included triples in my programme for the first time in international competition, finishing sixth in the long free and so pulling up to a final eleventh. It all went fairly well in the circumstances – no falls, and I managed to get through the programme without too much agony.

On arrival home, I went to the local hospital and had the ankle X-rayed. They said it was only a very bad sprain, that I should just rest it for a few days and that there should be no problem about going to Munich to compete in the World Championships.

Accordingly, I rested for a few days before going back to London to resume training and to get myself in condition for Munich, where the skating was to be held in the same arena that had been used for Olympic swimming two years earlier.

Having had a few problems with my ankle in London, I arrived in Munich and it started to play up again, so I had to scratch from the competition. It was the first really big disappointment in my skating career – withdrawal from my very first World Championship.

After returning from Munich, the ankle was again X-rayed and examined by specialists, who informed me that there was a slight chip on the ankle bone and that whoever had told me to continue to skate had been ill-advised; that I should not have been skating at all from the time I arrived back from Zagreb.

My ankle was duly strapped and I had to rest and wait. It was nearly six more weeks before the whole thing was cleared up and back to normal.

The season's major international contests in North America drew forty-seven skaters from twelve nations to the second Skate Canada meeting, in October, 1974, at the 6000-seat Memorial Auditorium in Kitchener, Ontario. With nothing to lose and plenty to gain, Cousins skated his rocker too fast, but settled to trace his other figures with greater control. His tenth place in the figures was perhaps a little lower than anticipated, but after the short free he rose three places to seventh.

The event was won decisively by the leading home entrant, Ron Shaver, and Cousins ended on a high note. Although sixth overall, he was third highest scorer in the free skating, a fight-back pattern that was to become familiar during the next two or three seasons.

At Richmond in the British Championships of December, 1974, Cousins was by far the most experienced of Curry's three challengers. The champion gained a substantial advantage in the figures, but, in the short free, Cousins excelled with a high double axel in his combination and was by no means overshadowed. Curry gained his fourth title in five years after engaging in a 'private' duel of courageous jumping with Cousins, a very worthy runner-up.

The European Championships in January, 1975, took place in Copenhagen's Brondby Hall, the largest indoor sports complex in Denmark. Eleventh in the figures, Cousins opened his short free with a great flying sit spin, but dropped marks when skid-landing an axel jump. Although not attempting a triple in the long free, he skated strongly throughout with no major errors to finish overall eleventh, but had the satisfaction of being placed the eighth best free skater.

Back to Canada – Kitchener, Ontario, this time – for Skate Canada '74 and, for me, a big improvement on the previous year's event; overall sixth and third place in the free skating. This was the start of my better performances and for the first time I was beginning to merit serious attention for my free skating. I felt this was a big step forward in my career and indeed the first major international in which I finished among the top three in free.

The British Championships of December, 1974, were again at Richmond and once more I was runner-up to John Curry, but getting closer all the time. John was a comfortable first and I was a comfortable second, but the margin was clearly narrower and there seemed a good chance that, within a couple of years,

41

I could be fighting John for a title that he had now held for three years in succession and for a fourth time in five seasons.

Following the British, I was selected for the European and World Championships in 1975, in Copenhagen and Colorado Springs respectively.

Four or five days prior to leaving for Copenhagen, I picked up a flu bug, like two or three other members of the British team, and perhaps because of this I remained eleventh, as in the previous year's European Championships.

For the fifth time in eighteen years, the World Championships were staged, in March, 1975, at the Broadmoor World Arena, Colorado Springs, most attractively sited, six thousand feet up and set beneath the steeply rising Rocky Mountains. Robin Cousins, at seventeen the British men's second string, traced smoother figures with greater confidence than at Copenhagen in January. Pulling up from fifteenth in the figures to finish twelfth of twenty-two, he featured a great triple salchow and an outstanding lay-over spin.

On to Colorado Springs, Colorado, USA, for – at last – my first World Championships, without any complications at all and a heartening overall eleventh place, including a sixth in the long programme. I was gradually creeping up the scale and things had started to come right again. People were beginning to be impressed and even American and Canadian journalists were using my name in their reports, so something must have been happening.

Colorado Springs was my first taste of American life and US skating. The luxurious Broadmoor, where we were staying, is a unique complex inasmuch as there are skiing, skating, swimming, golf and other sports facilities adjacent to a fabulous hotel in a picturesque mountain setting. And the American skating system appealed to me already.

We were using three skating rinks for training – the United States Air Force Academy rink, the Broadmoor Arena and also the smaller Broadmoor rink normally used for curling and, on this occasion, available for figures practice.

I was looked after at these Broadmoor events by Ronnie Baker, an English professional at the Broadmoor and a former partner of Gladys Hogg. We went to Denver twice to get extra training at the suburban rink there which is owned by Norma and Wally Sahlin, Charlie Tickner's tutors. Charlie still had not made the US world team, but had competed with me in a French international competition at St Gervais. Little did I know that, within a few years, he was going to be one of my biggest rivals.

John Curry wins his last British title, in 1975, with third-placed Glyn Jones on the right

4
My First Olympics

International figure skating in April 1975 moved to a less familiar continent for the Skate Safari meeting at Johannesburg's rooftop Sky Rink in the ultra-modern Carlton Centre. Watched by fascinated crowds who had never seen skating of such high standard, the meeting brought a memorable early confrontation between Cousins and the American, Charles Tickner, who held a slender advantage after the figures.

In the middle of the event, Cousins erred when combining double axel and double loop jumps, thus losing a little more ground, but he stole the thunder in a worthy finale. The steadily improving Bristol skater included a perfectly landed triple salchow and a brilliant combination of triple toe loop and double axel jumps in the best free skating performance of his career so far.

But although Cousins was a comfortable top-scorer in the free, he lost narrowly overall to Tickner, the vote of the five judges going 3–2 in the American's favour.

Almost immediately after arriving home from Colorado Springs, I found myself being put on a South African Airways plane to Johannesburg, to compete in that city's second international competition and the first to be called Skate Safari. Various national associations had been invited to send teams, to compete in Johannesburg and then, after a safari tour around the Kruger National Park, to go on a tour of other South African cities.

I was thrilled at being asked to go such a long way from home and to such a beautiful place as South Africa. It seems such a tragedy that the people there should be troubled by so much political controversy.

The competition was very well organized and, for the second time, I came up against Charlie, the eventual winner. I was placed second, but had the satisfaction of winning both the short and long free skating programmes. Thus, I collected one gold and two silver medals – for winning the free, coming second in the figures and second overall. It was my first senior international medal for figures and my first international free skating gold. So what started out as a competition which I was expected just to go and enjoy, without any expectations, ended up as a very rewarding international medal 'picker-upper'.

The tour afterwards took us to some beautiful places. We had four days in Durban to spend on the beach before our first exhibition show at the local rink, followed by similarly fascinating visits to Port Elizabeth, Pretoria and Cape Town.

Whilst still in South Africa, after the competition was over, I experienced the first twinges in my knee, which grew progressively worse. It was my right knee, the landing knee for nearly all my jumps.

Soon after I had returned home from South Africa and resumed training, I realized that every time I bent my knee it made a snapping noise, like someone walking over a bunch of dead twigs. This led to my second consultation with Les Bardsley, the Bristol City Football Club physiotherapist, who thought that I might have some sign of cartilage trouble and wanted to check it.

A specialist surgeon, Dr Clough, also said he was pretty sure it was the cartilage. At the time, I was finding it increasingly impossible to skate. Every time I bent my knee it would lock, maybe slightly, and there would be an enormous crack or snap before it got back into place.

I had my operation during the Wimbledon tennis fortnight of 1975 and, sure enough, the cartilage began to rip and I think that, if I had left it much later, the operation would not have been so successful. As it happened, with Les's expert help in physiotherapy and my own hard work – swimming, running, jogging and general exercising – it was less than ten weeks before I was back on the ice, preparing for the coming competition season, which was to be an Olympic one.

The first time I had seen Les Bardsley was the previous year, with the ankle problem, and on the recommendation of Pam Davies, who had seen him when a skater had cut her leg with a blade. My respect for his highly specialized knowledge of sports injuries was to grow even more as time progressed.

In the British Championships at Richmond in December, 1975, John Curry was aiming for his fourth consecutive men's title and his fifth in six years. Curry made a solid start, forging ahead to a commanding position at the end of the figures. It seemed all over bar the shouting. Then Cousins, his main challenger, narrowed the gap with a superior performance in the short free skating.

Cousins excelled when combining triple and double toe loop jumps, but Curry did not attempt a triple, erred on his double axel and did not spin as well as we knew he could.

In the opening seconds of his long free programme, Curry fell heavily and stared at the ice in disbelief before continuing, later avenging the lapse with great triple salchow and triple loop jumps. Cousins, who achieved four triple jumps, beat

45

Curry in the free skating to finish a much closer overall runner-up than anyone had anticipated. Would anyone in the audience then have predicted that Curry would win the three most prestigious international titles within the next eight weeks?

The European Championships of 1976, at the Patinoire des Vernets in Geneva, were like a final dress-rehearsal for the Innsbruck Olympics, due only a month later. John Curry, runner-up the year before, was in with a title chance. Cousins, eleventh in 1975, had subsequently improved so much that this very promising British second string who had landed four triples in the national championship five weeks previously, was expected to finish appreciably higher this time. Glyn Jones completed Britain's best male trio for years.

Cousins came thirteenth in the figures, the quality of his tracings showing a considerable improvement from the previous season. Seventh highest in the short free, Cousins agreeably surprised many who had not seen him for a year. He performed each element without error, correctly landing a superbly timed combination of triple and double toe loop jumps.

While Curry went on to become the first British European Champion for thirty-seven years, Cousins, who included four triples in the long free, ended overall sixth to complete a very happy day for his country, serving to remind us that a worthy national heir-apparent was fast maturing.

The first competition after my operation and the first test for my knee was to be the British Championships of December, 1975. Really and truly, all I wanted to do was to get *through* the event and hope that I had recovered sufficiently to be selected for the 1976 European, Olympic and World Championships – all to be held within a fifty-four-day period in Geneva, Innsbruck and Gothenburg respectively.

On the morning of the nationals at Richmond, John was back for his second British since going to America to train with Carlo Fassi. John won the first two figures and I was second in each. Then I won the third figure, much to my surprise – one of my better attempts at tracing.

On the afternoon of the same day, we had the short free skating. Glyn Jones, the boy with whom I was then training at Queen's, had planned, like John and myself, to include a triple in the jump combination.

John was the first of the three of us to skate and, for some reason, he changed his combination and did an easier double-double – and made a slight error. I came on and skated an error-free programme and beat John in this section for the first time.

John did not seem quite himself. I had won one of the figures and the short free and suddenly realized that there was an opportunity to win the whole championship if I could produce a good final free performance the following night.

We practised in the morning, John appearing to skate quite well and I was happy with my own form. Drawn to skate first of the three leaders, I proceeded

Home from Innsbruck in 1976 after my first Winter Olympics, with an official souvenir

that evening to perform my best to date, pulling off more triples than had ever been accomplished in any competition in Britain. Five triple jumps; two triple salchows – one in combination with double loop, two triple toe loops and a triple loop. I achieved better marks than ever before and all eyes turned to John to see what he could do.

Unfortunately, he took a fall in his opening triple jump and never seemed to regain his confidence, making two or three other errors. So I won the long free as well as the short free and knew the final reckoning had to be very, very close. I believe, in the overall result, less than three marks split the two of us and John must have breathed a deep sigh of relief when he knew he had retained the title.

All three of us – John, Glyn and myself – were selected for the three internationals to follow. It was going to be interesting to see how each of us would fare. In the meantime, John went back to America to resume training (I wonder how many anticipated what glory was in store for him). I had a pleasant, easy Christmas at home, preparing physically and mentally for the three big events to come.

In the Geneva Europeans, John showed that he had put everything together and I have never seen him skate better. He won the overall gold medal and gave British skating the biggest boost it had had for a very long time. I was quite happy with my final sixth place, proving that I was still moving up the scale. I came fourth in the free skating, when one or two judges placed me second behind John.

The tension during the compulsory figures at the 1976 Innsbruck Olympics was heightened by unusually meticulous scrutiny of the figure tracings, several judges getting down on all fours to examine the rocker turns – and sometimes methodically pacing out the dimensions of each circle.

Geoffrey Yates, the British judge, several times lay full length on the ice and it seemed that only the magnifying glass and deerstalker were missing from the Holmesian image.

Fourteenth in the figures, Cousins rose two places to twelfth after a spectacular short free performance without blemish, and notable for excellent spins as well as a clever linkage of triple and double toe loop jumps.

Finally finishing tenth, Cousins cleanly landed no fewer than five triple jumps in the long free, also underlining his growing versatility in spins. If ever Cousins was undermarked in a major championship, this was it, and no doubt British criticism of his marks would have been greater had it not been for the ecstasy of Curry's gold medal triumph.

The 1976 Olympic Winter Games in Innsbruck was the biggest sporting occasion I had experienced. We arrived at the Olympic village, which was surrounded by armed guards, police and dogs, and settled into our British flat. All the skaters were housed in the same apartment-type building, with the national flag outside indicating its occupants. The men's skating was one of the later events scheduled, so this gave us a little time to get interested in some of the other competitions and general activities around.

It was difficult actually to go and see many of the other events. Most of the skiing was being held too far away, but we did get to visit the ski jumping, which was incredible to watch 'live,' and also managed to watch the British bob-sledders during practice.

Every facility that you could reasonably want was laid on for the competitors. There were shops, a cinema, games rooms, music – all collectively providing, for three-and-a-half weeks, the biggest thrill I had encountered. The competitions sometimes seemed almost incidental because everyone was having such fun in their leisure time. In these circumstances, the atmosphere stayed very relaxed right the way through.

The results came out the same for John as at Geneva – another win and an even bigger boost for Britain. I finished overall tenth in my first Olympics, producing what I think was my best free skating up to that time – with the same triples in a programme similar to that skated in the British at Richmond. No opponent equalled my five triples, not even John, yet I only managed to place eighth in the free skating.

Held less than a month after the glamorous Winter Games, the World Champion-ships in an Olympic year are usually somewhat anti-climactic and those at Gothen-burg in 1976 were no exception in this respect. It was certainly a tame end to the season for Cousins, though he finished a commendable ninth. After two of his final five minutes had elapsed, the lace of one of his boots came loose and, instead of jumping five triples, as in Innsbruck, he could manage only two.

One of the first to congratulate Curry when his compatriot completed the triple crown, Cousins was already being widely tipped to follow in his footsteps. It seemed quite conceivable that in Cousins – eight years younger – Britain might possess the potential Olympic gold medallist of 1980. True, his figure tracings remained an encumbrance, but this was a weakness one felt sure he would now strive assiduously to remedy.

On to Gothenburg for the 1976 World Championships and John's third inter-national title – and ninth place for me, an improvement of one place on the Olympics. Unfortunately, two minutes through my long free skating routine, a lace started to come unravelled on one of my skates. It did not come down low enough to impair my skating by dragging close to the blades, but it did affect me slightly towards the end of the programme as it was getting looser and looser and I could feel my ankle beginning to wobble a little.

However, I managed to get through without any mistakes and nobody seemed to notice but myself that the lace had come undone. So the winter ended on a promising note. John announced his retirement and I knew more eyes would be focussed on me the following season.

Cousins was a leading topic of conversation in Ottawa when he arrived with the rest of the British team to compete in the fourth Skate Canada at the Civic Centre in October 1976. A distinguished field included seven of the top fifteen in the last World Championships. After the three compulsory figures, Ron Shaver, representing the host country, led Igor Bobrin of USSR by a 4–3 assessment of the judges. Third was the American, David Santee, with Cousins fourth.

The issue obviously rested between these tightly-bunched four, with Bobrin the least likely to triumph, the figures being regarded as his major strength. This was the first big test to determine who might fill the void created by the retirement of Curry and the Canadian Toller Cranston, the two who had set the sport alight in the previous season with their insistence on making free skating an art form.

How lasting their influence would be, or whether the men would revert to the more traditional athleticism, which is dynamic and exciting in a different way, became more apparent in this event. Cousins, making his third Skate Canada appearance, was developing his own distinctive style and it was felt that much that he and Shaver did during the coming months might, instead, shape the future technique of men's free skating.

Cousins rose to second after the short free despite missing a triple loop jump. In the final free, Shaver opened with three triple toe loop jumps and later included a triple loop in a programme good enough to maintain his earlier lead. An impressive runner-up, Cousins, although attempting less than usual, made no error and the judges, through their marks, left no doubt that they considered the tall young Englishman's style of presentation superior, awarding him the only maximum six given.

A British all-round resurgence was completed by spirited performances from Karena Richardson, who set a well-informed crowd buzzing with appreciation for her strong finish behind local girl Kim Alletson; and from Warren Maxwell and Janet Thompson, who all but wrested ultimate glory in the ice dancing from their Soviet victors, Gennadi Karponosov and Natalia Linichuk. Three silver medals for Britain were secured, each against opposition of sufficient quality to justify national jubilation.

The 1976–77 season began for me with the Skate Canada competition in Ottawa in October. An overall second place was achieved – my best result so far in this event. Fourth in figures put me well in the running for a medal, then

Runner-up to Ron Shaver, of the host country, in the 1976 Skate Canada international competitions in Ottawa, with American David Santee third

second in both the short and long programmes gave me an advantage over the American, David Santee, and the Russian, Igor Bobrin, and I finished runner-up behind the Canadian Champion and favourite, Ronnie Shaver.

Skate Canada '76 was my first international competition as the British number one. Since John's retirement, I had, as it were, unofficially replaced him, though we would have to wait until the Nationals at Richmond in December to see whether or not I was going to be his successor.

Skate Canada has always been a great competition in every way. You find yourself very relaxed because the atmosphere is so friendly. On this occasion, between the compulsory figures, I was standing by the barrier and having a conversation with Ronnie Shaver about eating and what I had brought with me from the Ottawa Holiday Inn, where we were all staying, to eat when peckish while waiting off the ice.

We ended with a humorous argument about how the English and North American words differ in meaning. For example, what we would call the boot of a car, they would call the trunk, our bonnet is their hood, and so on. After a while, we suddenly realized that here we were in the middle of a big, dramatic competition, arguing over the English language.

A Canadian lady standing nearby found it most amusing to listen to the two of us – earnest rivals on the ice – talking like this. We also discussed the usage of words like buns, pastries, cakes, cookies and gateaux, when I happened to mention currants and sultanas. Well, this lady started laughing very hard – and the following morning in my mail box at the hotel I found a little package which contained a very small packet of currants from this lady, who had been much amused by our conversation and had broken the tension for the two of us.

That was a characteristic personal experience of the Canadian people and their involvement with the British skaters. Skate Canada in Ottawa was to be the beginning of my special relationship with the Canadian people and the Canadian press – and every time since when I have competed in Canada, I have always had an excellent reception and, as I have mentioned elsewhere, it is just as if I am skating at home.

5
Knee Deep in Trouble

The highly probable winner looked well entrenched halfway through the British men's championship at Richmond in December, 1976. Cousins, tracing his three compulsory figures with greater accuracy and better style than previously, gained an early commanding advantage, afterwards consolidated in the initial free skating. Though wincing from pain as he marred his jump combination, he made only that one error and all but eliminated any lingering fears that the newly healed little toe he broke only three weeks previously could affect the outcome in the final round.

Encouraged by coachloads of his home town supporters, Robin Cousins proved his mettle at Richmond, demonstrating the highest degree of technical ability and entertaining footwork. He also showed a true champion's spirit. This likeable, shy yet daring performer was in great pain after landing from a triple salchow on a badly bruised toe and he was rewarded with a six for artistic impression.

Even without attempting his originally intended triple lutz, the new National Champion finished with plenty in hand over his closest rival, Glyn Jones, who won a tense duel for second place with Andrew Bestwick.

Richmond, December 1976, and my first British Championship without John seemed very strange. For three years I had gone to each event looking up to him, and now everyone was coming to Richmond to look at me. The British public and press had an enormous boost from John's triple crown victories, and somehow it seemed that they expected me to jump straight into his shoes as European and World Champion.

Well, there was no way this was going to happen that early and I was a little apprehensive as to how people would react when they realized I was simply not capable of living up to their immediate expectations, and that the best that could be hoped for was a medal standing.

Two weeks before the Nationals, I had a small accident in my bedroom when, climbing across all my clutter, I stubbed the little toe of my right foot, which resulted in a breakage. I found it very difficult to skate properly for a good ten days and had to take out one or two triples from the programme. Fortunately, this little episode did not leak out much before the event – those who did know advised me to take more water with it, so one can imagine how the media may have reacted.

Despite this frustration, which naturally caused some pre-championship anxiety, I more or less walked away with the British title that year, winning all three sections, and put myself in a good position for the forthcoming European and World Championships in Helsinki and Tokyo.

Vladimir Kovalev, the Soviet Union's Olympic silver medallist, narrowly led Jan Hoffmann of East Germany, the 1974 winner, when the 1977 European Championships began at the Helsinki Ice Hall. Kovalev, whose temperamental misbehaviour had brought suspension from the Russian team a couple of years back, was now a reformed character, a model of calm concentration.

The grandeur of nearby Finlandia Hall was matched by the graceful dignity of Hoffmann's meticulous patterns. The East German had a commanding presence comparable to that of cricketer Geoff Boycott in full flow. Cousins began with a well-controlled counter figure, which earned sixth highest marks, then lost a little ground in the paragraph bracket before ending with a sounder paragraph loop.

Seventh in the figures was six places higher than at the same stage of this event the previous season. Significantly, he showed that he was beginning to master a tendency to rush his figures, and that boded well for the future. But the accuracy of his tracings had yet to reach fruition, and his many British fans, eager for another triumph of Curry dimensions, would have to be patient; it would be grossly unfair to expect too much of him too soon.

Relieved from the figure chores he liked the least, Cousins really came alive in the short free skating session which tested each competitor's ability in seven prescribed elements. Brilliantly linking triple toe loop and double loop jumps, Cousins landed a perfect double lutz and demonstrated just what a great spinner he had become – fast and versatile.

He scored the second highest marks of the day, bettered only by Hoffmann, leaping three places to fourth from overnight seventh. On the final night, Cousins overhauled local boy Pekka Leskinen to clinch the bronze medal. Each of his jumps was supremely landed in a manner to suggest he just did not know how to fall. But he only included one triple – the toe loop – perhaps wisely opting for caution, to score the highest marks of all for presentation; five judges awarded him 5·9, enough to gain a supplementary silver medal as second best free skater in the event. Hoffmann recaptured the title he had held in 1974, setting too high an overall standard for Kovalev to eclipse, the Russian's chance evaporating when he fell attempting a triple loop.

The first World Figure Skating Championships to be staged in Asia took place in

With Karena Richardson (left) and Tracey Solomons in an ice pantomine at
Altrincham in 1976

March, 1977, at the Yoyogi National Stadium, Tokyo, which had been the swimming venue for the 1964 summer Olympics. So far as Cousins was concerned, the occasion reflected his immense courage in adversity.

As in a cup final, the one who gets the break on the day goes into the record books. If nothing else, the annals will show that Robin Cousins, at the point when he was forced to withdraw, had already indicated what he might have achieved, had he not 'retired injured'.

The men's event was disappointing in other ways. Ron Shaver, suffering from a leg injury, finished an undistinguished sixth. Kovalev, the winner, though competent enough, seldom showed flair in his performance. Hoffmann, who lost narrowly, competed despite a heavy cold which must have sapped his stamina.

Back in his room at Tokyo's luxurious Keio Plaza, the tallest hotel in Asia, Robin turned his gaze from the snow-capped Mount Fujiyama, ruefully rubbed his then famous left knee and said: 'I'll be all right before next season starts.'

At the 1977 European Championships in Helsinki, there seemed a reasonable chance of my getting a medal if I skated my best and I felt keenly that it was up to me to take over from John Curry as British Champion by doing as good a job as was humanly possible.

By personal standards, I skated good figures, coming seventh in that part of the competition – the first time I had made the top ten in figures in Europe. I went on to skate good enough short and long programmes to come away with the supplementary silver medal for free skating and the overall bronze – my first medals in the European Championships.

I came home from Helsinki elated and looking forward to leaving for Tokyo, hopefully to gain a World Championship medal there, but life was beginning to go too smoothly. . . .

Early one Sunday morning at the Bristol rink, I was warming up on the ice when, suddenly – crunch. It was my left knee, exactly the same problem that I had had with my right knee, only much worse, and that was it – or was it?

I had to be carried off the ice and, very soon afterwards, I was on the phone to Les Bardsley. Could I come up straight from the rink and see him because I couldn't even straighten my knee? It had locked in the bent position. There was no doubt this time that it was the cartilage and that it would take a manipulatory operation that afternoon to straighten the knee out again. I felt on grimly familiar ground going back to the hospital with Dr Clough, who, thankfully, was available at the time to do the operation.

Did this mean Tokyo was off? According to the two medical men, it was going to be hard enough for me just to walk around without the knee collapsing again. But I wanted to skate and I was determined to skate in the Tokyo World Championships.

56

So Les Bardsley came to the rink with me one day and we strapped it and worked on it and tried various strappings to see which gave the best support. It was not easy, a tedious case of trial and error; once or twice the strapping did not suit and it took three weeks before I could finally skate.

But I was still utterly resolved to go to Tokyo and compete there. Then I received a letter from my National Association to say that they had heard about the accident and that I planned to go to Tokyo with no intention of competing and just to have a good time! This made me even more determined to put up a good performance.

Somehow, they had wind of an erroneous idea that I intended to bide my time, go to Tokyo and, once I reached this fantastic place, just withdraw from the event and enjoy myself. In fact, I was even informed that, should I go to Tokyo and withdraw at any time during the first two days of the competition, I would end up having to pay for the trip myself.

I was going to Tokyo with no intention of withdrawing at all and had already decided that I would be working with Carlo Fassi in Tokyo to see how we fared together, with a view, maybe, to spending the summer with him in Denver, Colorado.

In this confused atmosphere, I arrived in Tokyo and started practising, but without using all the practice time allowed. I went to the draw with my fingers crossed, hoping that they would draw the group I knew I was capable of performing without risking further damage to the knee.

In this respect at least, Fortune smiled. I was lucky enough to have not only the most suitable group of figures, but also the right foot drawn. This meant that only one of my figures would have to be started on the bad leg.

I skated adequately, so far as my figures were concerned, finishing ninth in the compulsories. Meantime, I had changed around my short free programme plans, at least in my mind, reversing practically all the elements from my left foot to the right – something nobody normally does.

I had decided to take the triple out and make a very much easier double jump combination. The flying sit spin I had taught myself to do on the other foot, which for me was the wrong foot, but it seemed the wisest course.

But I had done well enough in the figures to reason that, if anything was going to happen to my knee, it would happen regardless of how I was skating. So, I told myself, forget what you have altered and just do the programme as it should be done.

I got out on the ice to warm up for the short programme, skated around and – clink – right in the middle of the warm-up, my knee gave out. The watching German, Dr Montag, who was close at hand, re-strapped the knee for me but strapped it so tightly that I could hardly bend it.

'This will never give out,' he said. I decided OK, fair enough, the knee's collapsed already. If it's going to happen, it's going to happen, so just get out there and do your thing.

For some reason, I decided on the spur of the moment that, as my knee had already given out and was supposedly strapped so that it would not happen again, I would put the triple in – and successfully accomplished it.

The flying sit spin was the last element of the seven in my programme, so, I reasoned, it won't matter. If it cracks, it will crack in a sit spin position and I'll just stay down there forever and the judges can please themselves what they do.

As it happened, I just literally forgot about the other foot idea and did the flying sit spin as I normally do it – on the left foot, on the bad leg, and somehow managed to come out of it unscathed, apart from my knee feeling as if it were blowing up like a balloon.

In reality, I skated a near-perfect programme and came off in absolute agony – but also with first places from two of the nine judges, and thus I pulled up to the top six in the world at that stage of the event.

How I got through that programme, I shall never know, but I was afterwards even more determined to finish the long programme the following day. (Incidentally, I had been advised before the trip that an operation after returning would be done in any case and that no long-term damage was likely in the meantime).

Below and opposite Going for a spin in Helsinki, 1977

58

My knee collapsed four times during one forty-five minute practice session the following morning, but still determined to go on, I went again to the doctor prior to the long free to get my knee re-strapped.

Dr Montag, my brother Martin and Howard Bass watched anxiously from a few feet away as I loosened up before going on for the 'make-or-break' long programme. The music began, I started and all seemed well until, about two minutes through the performance, when I was doing one of the simplest of manoeuvres – just a basic turn – the knee collapsed. I straightened up and threw myself into a camel spin, hoping that the force of my leg being thrown backwards would jar the knee back into position.

Well, as I finished the spin and went to step on the leg, I realized that was it. There was no leg there to stand on. I just collapsed in a heap in the middle of the ice and literally crawled off to the side; the British team leader, Eileen Anderson, ran around to the referee and officially withdrew me at that point – just three minutes under the required time.

If for only three minutes more my knee could have held out, I should have been able to complete the Championship. It was not to be, but at least I tried.

Four days after leaving Tokyo, I found myself once more in St Mary's Hospital in Bristol, this time for my second cartilage operation, which was to be more successful than the first. Not only was it easier for Dr Clough to do the operation, but easier to recover, having already once gone through the training and the hard work to get my other knee back in peak condition.

I knew by now how hard I could work, how hard I could push and what I could not push, and within seven-and-a-half weeks I was back walking normally and doing basic skating. Within nine weeks of the operation, I was in America again, skating in a club ice show in Denver.

I was extremely lucky to have Les Bardsley's expert help. He is an excellent physiotherapist and, after receiving a glowing recommendation, I took to him the first time around. It cannot be so easy when one is more accustomed to treating rugby players, soccer players and cricketers. The difference in my field of sport and theirs is quite considerable and the first operation preceded much trial and error in recuperation regarding what I could and could not do.

The second time around, therefore, we were able to use this experience to my advantage, insofar as we could progress much faster and push it maybe that little bit harder the second time, especially after Les had been to the rink and seen more for himself what was required of the knee in skating action. So, we were soon some two weeks further ahead with progress than the first time. Without Les's highly specialized advice, I am sure it would have taken a good many months to regain full fitness.

6
Ice Time Problems

The underlying reason why Curry and Cousins went abroad to train, why Karena Richardson left London to prepare in Wales before also going abroad, and why other top British skaters have felt obliged to practise at very unsociable hours, sometimes after midnight, is because Britain, and London in particular, possesses far too few ice rinks to satisfy all needs. This situation dates from the Fifties, when large ice stadia at Brighton, Earls Court and Harringay were swallowed up in lucrative property developments and the Wembley rink became a valuable site for other uses.

Surprisingly, there are still fewer than forty rinks throughout Britain – nearly half of them in Scotland, where curling claims the lion's share of ice time. France, a fair comparison, has more than a hundred rinks and, while there are only four in the greater London area, Paris has fifteen.

No ice sport in Great Britain can expand much more without additional civic rinks, which can more than pay their way when properly managed. The demand is surely comparable with that for swimming pools and, if these are installed adjacently, costs can be trimmed by using a complementary power plant to freeze the ice and heat the water.

With civic lotteries now permitted to raise funds for such enterprises, there could and should be an indoor ice rink in every large town, suitable for skaters, curlers and ice hockey players and with adequate spectator accommodation to make it all viable. In the meantime ice is so precious for public sessions that too little time or space is available for proper international training requirements.

Before I started to win senior competitions – that is to say, before I took over John Curry's national title – I had been very much a runner-up and a secondary skater. Then, when I became British Champion, it quickly occurred to me that people were going to want me to win competitions consistently. Yet how can we in Britain begin to win international events when the facilities and the conditions that we are training under are not really conducive to any type of international competition whatsoever?

When I was skating in Bristol, it was early morning and evening sessions. When I started to train in Queen's Ice Club in London, it was even earlier in the morning and, to my way of thinking, you simply cannot properly attain top championship level if you have to train continually at six or seven o'clock in the morning.

We were also having to fight to find time in public sessions. We could skate during the public sessions provided that not too many kids came in and there were no school classes that day. What kind of preparation is that for a would-be world-beater?

When you go abroad, you listen and talk to other skaters and competitors and they tell you how much ice they are using and how long each day they are getting for training. It is very disheartening, to say the least, and you really begin to wonder if you are wasting your time.

I had been approached by a few people and asked why I did not go out to spend some weeks training at this place or the other place, but, of course, it is much easier said than done.

After John had won all his medals and I had been talking to him about this problem, he mentioned that the best part of his amateur career had been the last two years, when he had been in Denver with Carlo Fassi, and he just wished he had been able to do it earlier.

I had an appropriate opportunity to discuss this with Carlo and he invited me to train with him in Denver, Colorado. Until he made the suggestion, I had been getting quite frustrated with the British training problems. Perhaps it was a bit selfish, but I wanted to give myself more scope and Denver really seemed the ultimate for me. The opportunity I had been offered was really too good to turn down.

Carlo Fassi was Italian men's champion in 1943 and Italian pairs champion from 1942 to 1954. He was European men's champion in 1953 and 1954 and world bronze medallist in 1953.

Gregory R. Smith, former editor of *Skating*, official magazine of the United States Figure Skating Association, wrote of Fassi:

'He is one of the most successful coaches in modern figure skating history. Among his students before Cousins have been Olympic and World Champions, Peggy Fleming, Dorothy Hamill and John Curry.

'A skater, according to Fassi, must be an athlete; quick and powerful, with a lot of ability and balance. He must be intelligent. "But skating is not all athletics – it is also an art," he says. "The choreography is much more important now than it was."

'He seems to have a knack for recognizing and developing championship talent. He said, "I am lucky, I get along with kids. I get along with friendships and under-standing; rapport is natural. I have order and discipline and I get it by assuming that's the way it goes. Communicating is the key. With a top skater you can't yell and scream; by that time, he can do it or he can't but don't waste practice."

'Part of Fassi's ground rules prohibit displays of emotion on the ice. He said the students "must keep cool on the ice. It isn't easy sometimes," he added with a smile, "to get senior ladies together."

'Another important factor in Fassi's training is the equality shown each student. There is "no special preference, and the kids feel it if there is. I try to be impartial with everyone. The pro must totally support the kids skating and the skaters must know that the pro is there."

'It is inspiration provided by good skaters training together (and against each other, too) that Fassi supervises and uses to improve his students' technical and artistic skating ability.

'He described Curry as "a unique, aristocratic and sophisticated skater," but said that Cousins, "a happy-go-lucky skater," has more talent.'

Training in London would begin on early morning ice which was reserved exclusively for Gladys's pupils. This provided free skating for me, before my figures practice, from maybe 6 a.m. or 6.30 until 8 a.m. Then we would have a compulsory figures patch from 8.30 to 9.30. The following half-hour again would be Gladys's ice, which we would use for running through programmes before the public session began at 10 a.m.

During that public session, from 10 until noon, what skating we did would depend on how many members of the public were in, whether the schools came in and if the ends of the ice were roped off. If it was a period when schools were on holiday, then that would be two hours that we would lose.

Lunchtimes would be taken up by a second compulsory figures patch, starting as soon as the ice was dry (after re-surfacing) at around 12.30 and continuing till 2 p.m. That would be more or less it for the day. It meant going to bed very early, for me usually between 8.30 and 9 p.m. – sometimes earlier if I was going to get up at 5 to get to the rink by 6 a.m.

This unenviable timetable meant that we were training or running through championship routines and generally completing most of our serious practice before ten in the morning – rather strange considering competitions often end after ten in the evening.

In Denver, I would do three compulsory figure patches in succession, from 8 until 11.30 in the morning. Then I would have an hour's free skating through the lunchtime, usually from 11.30 or noon until 1 o'clock. The afternoons would be free, then I would be back again in the early evenings to do more compulsory figures work from 6 to 7 p.m., followed by another hour's free skating.

So, summing up the difference, in England I would be lucky to get up to two-and-a-half hours' figures work and between one and two hours' free skating each day, whereas in America I had from five to six hours for figures and another three for free skating.

In England, I used to train from Monday through to Friday in London and would come home at weekends whenever possible and skate in Bristol, on Saturday from 7 a.m. until 8 a.m. and at Sunday lunchtime from 1 o'clock until 2 p.m. My training in America has averaged six hours a day from Mondays to Fridays, with Saturdays off and three hours' skating on Sunday from 10 a.m. until 1 p.m. Not only were the periods available longer, but at more sociable hours and on less densely populated ice.

When I trained in London I was, of course, obliged to move from Bristol, so lived in a small 'bed-sitter' – a one-room place in Notting Hill Gate, just five minutes' walking distance from the rink. In Denver, I was fortunate to be able to live with the Wylie family and it was much easier – a sort of home-from-home arrangement. It made a great difference having someone there to look after me, in contrast to the somewhat lonely life in London when I was not at the rink.

Fifty of the world's top figure skaters gathered for the fifth annual Skate Canada meeting in October, 1977, at the Moncton Coliseum in New Brunswick. The fact that twenty-six of the entrants had finished among the top fifteen of their respective events in the last World Championships underlined the status which this leading non-championship international series had already achieved.

The absence, for the first time, of a Canadian men's contender with a serious chance – Toller Cranston and Ron Shaver both having turned professional – prompted local support to switch emphatically to Cousins, who had finished a close runner-up to Shaver the previous year. Few British skaters before can have acquired such a fervent following abroad as that which Cousins was now enjoying.

Before the competition began, Cousins had said how much he felt his technique in figures had advanced during summer training. He proceeded to prove it in no uncertain manner.

Cousins and Charles Tickner, the US National Champion from Littleton, Colorado, were neck and neck after the opening phase. At the end of the three compulsory figures, Tickner led by a 5–4 assessment of the judges, though the British skater had scored fractionally more points. A marked progress in the notably careful and more deliberate Cousins' tracings was apparent from the start. Never before ahead at this stage of a major international contest, he was, to all intents and purposes, level with Tickner.

The ease with which Cousins finally ousted Tickner in the free skating was very reassuring. It seemed incredible that he had had a cartilage removed only seven

Carlo Fassi and I agree with the judges' marks at the 1977 European Championships in Helsinki

months previously. He included two brilliant triple jumps, yet skated well within himself. His flying sit spin, which put so much pressure on the knee in question, looked better than ever.

Tickner, himself renowned for triples, tried to pull out all the stops in a desperate effort to make up his deficit after the short free, but he was no match for Cousins this time. So Britain secured two gold medals, the other going to ice dancers Warren Maxwell and Janet Thompson.

Skate Canada '77, in October at Moncton, New Brunswick, was my first international with my new coach, Carlo Fassi, and it was going to be an important test to see how we would work together during a competition. It is one thing working with a professional when training, but quite another to be able to work together when actually at a competition and under all the pressures which inevitably build up in that atmosphere.

Well, everything went fine and was plain sailing. We had a great time there. It was not only Carlo and myself. There were nine other international skaters from his Denver camp, all competing in their respective events. So we were one little happy family, one little band of skaters who worked together and watched each other train and practise.

The compulsory figures came as a bit of a shock to me, but an agreeable one. I think for the first time I proved to myself that I could do figures in competition as well as I could in practice, which is what I had spent most of my year working on in Denver. Carlo was very happy, I was very happy and the judges were very happy.

Although four of the nine judges placed me first, I finished second in the figures by a very small margin to Charlie Tickner, whom I had never before beaten or even been close to in a compulsory figures section. Taking a few firsts from him at this stage was therefore an achievement I had not anticipated.

I skated a technically good short programme and came off first in that section and now led Charlie in the event by a thread. Although it was a straightforward performance, I had not skated all seven elements quite as well as I was capable of doing. I had not 'shown off' at all and was quietly advised by a British official that, if I wanted to make a good impression in the long free the following day, I was going to have to give plenty more 'show'.

The final free skating practice was satisfactory and uneventful. No drama, no mishaps – quite a novel experience for me. We waited patiently for the final night.

To be honest, I skated what was probably one of my lowest competitive performances of my senior international career, barely doing everything I had to do and probably skating like a sack of potatoes. But most of the other skaters either made mistakes or did not perform particularly well either, so I came away yet again with the gold medal for free skating, and for the first time in an international event, the overall gold medal. Yes, I had beaten Charlie.

I am saying how I felt at the time. According to the press and most of the audience, I had skated a good programme and they were all very impressed. But, for myself, I just felt that I went out there and skated a performance because I had to, instead of drawing inspiration from having the crowd behind me. I did not really feel relaxed enough.

On reflection, I think it was the first time in an international event in which I was going into the final section already in first place and all of a sudden there was nowhere to go but down. I should have realized that I could have consolidated the lead more substantially. Instead, I lost all my usual bounce and flair and started to worry the whole way through the programme about losing my position.

It does not seem so bad to drop from fourth to fifth, but it always seems worse to fall from first to second. Luckily on this occasion, I managed to pull through and stay in front.

As a matter of interest, this was my fourth appearance in the five Skate Canada meetings since their inauguration – a distinction shared at the time only by that delightfully exotic Japanese girl, Emi Watanabe.

British skaters can always feel at home in Canada. The Canadian audiences have always had a soft spot for the British performers and this was especially notable in Moncton in 1976. At this time, all the previous Canadian national champions had retired, the team was in the midst of rebuilding and so there were no top Canadians seriously in the hunt for medals.

Consequently, the Canadian public more or less adopted the whole British team and it was almost as if we were skating in our home country with the roars of approval that we got from the spectators. We always felt greatly at home in Skate Canada and in all my appearances there I never once felt it was at all like a foreign country or that the people were not truly behind me.

7
A Close Call

Cousins returned from his American coaching base at Denver for the first defence of his title in the sixty-third British Championships, at Richmond in December, 1977. After unexpectedly conceding a tiny deficit to Andrew Bestwick in the figures, the defending Champion made easy work of the short free skating, featuring a spectacular flying sit spin as only he knew how and a superb linkage of triple and double toe loop jumps.

The judges had split 4–3 in Bestwick's favour after the holder's uncertain start, but Cousins later had every judge solidly behind him with a well-nigh flawless performance. His convincing retention of the title was later assured by a scintillating long free display, including three triples, and earning two sixes.

The British Championships at Richmond in December 1977 were a curious experience: returning home to England to defend the title for the first time. I had come fresh from my success in Moncton and, even more recently, had had two very successful performances, though only in exhibitions – one in Madison Square Gardens in the American Superskates Show and the other in the Boston Jimmy Fund Show.

I arrived in London refreshed and ready to show the British public and judges what improvement I had made during my past year in Denver. Practising was a little awkward at Richmond, mainly because everybody would practise compulsory figures at the same time – men and ladies – the overall low entries making this possible. Still, it was the same for everybody.

On the morning of the figures I felt good during the warm-up and Pam Davies was there to guide me. Suddenly, after first feeling eager to show everyone how well I could perform, I had this strange idea that some people were waiting to see me make a mistake and find fault because I had moved to America and put down training roots there.

It was, to say the least, unpleasant. I went from bad to worse and disaster followed disaster so that I finished a humiliating second in the compulsory figures section to Andrew Bestwick, a relatively unknown skater on the international circuit who was competing in only his second British Championships.

Andrew skated good figures, but there was no reason why I should not have won. I should have been able to walk away with the figures section. Instead, I went to pieces and things certainly did not turn out as expected.

Unfortunately, with a small entry there was insufficient time between each figure for competitors to take their boots off and relax before continuing. So gradually, as the three figures progressed, I became more and more tense and literally collapsed in a heap when the third figure had been completed – a kind of nervous exhaustion, I suppose.

Realizing what a stupid mistake I had made and that I had two more sections left, I resolved to forget about that unhappy morning and pick up the pieces. Less than three hours later, I produced what I considered to be my best short programme up to that time and shot into the lead.

The following morning, we were up bright and early for the last free skating practice. There had been a good media reaction and it seemed everybody was now waiting for me and rooting for me. That felt better, and I knew that I was going to have three or four coach-loads of my loyal supporters from Bristol arriving on the doorstep at Richmond that night.

I walked into the rink and everything was a-buzz. The special television roof lights were brightening the scene, the competition was already under way and the general excitement could be certainly felt.

Well, here we go again, let's show them what you can do, I pep-talked myself – and I did. For the first time in my career, I received a perfect six for technical merit. That felt good. I suppose I skated a near-flawless programme and was very, very well pleased with a result that managed to make everybody forget – and, one hopes, forgive – the silly mistakes I had made the day before.

Cousins rallied gamely after an uncertain start, to end the first day of the 1978 European Championships in Strasbourg in a handy fifth position. The big British hope looked ill-at-ease during the initial inside rocker figure and was marked a humiliating ninth. To his credit, he never lost composure and bounced back to place fourth in the middle figure, the forward outside paragraph three.

Moving from strength to strength, he traced the faster back change loop with supreme confidence and, for that, was adjudged third, the probable position he would have ended in the figures but for a crucial hesitant moment in that first tracing.

But fifth was still two places higher than he was at the corresponding stage of this event the previous season. This time, with less leeway to make up and a formidable and clearly improved free skating capacity, he remained very much in contention.

Cousins next day rose brilliantly to the occasion with appreciably the best performance in the short free programme of seven elements. Skilfully combining spectacular triple and double toe loop jumps and executing his flying sit spin as no other can, he received a maximum six mark from one judge and the best score of all in this part of the event, to move up to fourth place.

World Champion Vladimir Kovalev, who had led in the figures, was out-skated by Jan Hoffmann of East Germany and his own countryman, Igor Bobrin, as well as by Cousins. The Russian made his jump combination as difficult as buttering a croissant and failed even to attempt a triple.

So Kovalev relinquished his overnight lead to Hoffmann and Cousins was almost level with third-placed Bobrin. Britain's hope, now with little doubt the best free skater present, had perhaps narrowed the gap enough to scent possible victory. The stage was set for an absorbing climax, inevitably to be punctuated by higher and more daring jumps than ever.

Even the great veteran coach, Jacques Gerschwiler, gasped, 'This is too much,' when he watched tremendous leaps during the earlier practice. He could hardly believe what he saw to be physically possible.

Jan Hoffmann, at twenty-two, retained the title after an enthralling three-way tussle with Kovalev and Cousins. It was the East German's third victory, having first won in 1974 before cartilage complications kept him off the ice for a whole season.

Cousins, two years younger, narrowly failed to become the third Briton to win since the event began in 1893, his successful compatriots being Graham Sharp in 1939 and John Curry in 1976. But he proved beyond question to be the world's best free skater, outpointing everybody in a magnificent display of first-class spins and jumps, receiving better marks than the Champion from every judge.

Two perfect triple toe loops, one triple salchow and a slightly faulty triple loop were his highlights, gaining a six from the French judge for presentation and 5·9 from all the others.

If only Cousins had traced a better first figure on the opening day, the title would surely have been his. Plainly, he was destined for every top honour with just a little more attention to those tracings.

Hoffmann achieved three good triples, lutz, salchow and toe-loop, but over-rotated an attempted triple loop. Runner-up Kovalev, on his twenty-fifth birthday, had two triple salchows and a triple loop, but two-footed a triple toe loop and failed with a flying sit spin. Although third overall, Cousins of course received the supplementary gold medal as top free skater.

The European Championships of 1978, held in Strasbourg, France, found me hungry to get into the fray. It was my first international championship quest since training under Carlo in Denver and, for the first time, I felt ready and eager well in advance. I had a rather nasty fall during one of the practices, but, on the whole, the preparations went very smoothly.

We had one slight problem in one of the compulsory figures. Ironically, I

Trying not to be nervous while executing a championship figure under the critical eyes of the judges

had done so well during the warm-ups for the figures that there did not seem much that Carlo could say. Anyway, I did not concentrate on the first figure quite so much as I should have done. It was the left inside rocker and it went a little bit haywire.

I did manage afterwards to put down two of my best figures – the paragraph double three and the change loop. But the judges had already awarded me bad marks for the first figure and were not going to make up that much difference on the other two. Be that as it may, I am fairly sure that I could have done a little better.

I skated one of my best short programmes and one of the judges rewarded me with a six. I had had sixes before, but, except in the British Championships, this was the first six that I really think I was worth, certainly at international level. Thus boosted, I was ready and raring to go in the long programme, with a medal seemingly within reach.

In my own estimation, the long programme was technically adequate, but the presentation I knew was better and I enjoyed it probably more than any I had previously performed. The audience and judges seemed to like it too. I did make a slight error on the triple loop, but everyone else made mistakes as well, so I ended first in that section, thus gaining my second European bronze medal and, with it, another gold for the free skating.

The eight British figure skaters at the Civic Centre rink in Ottawa to contest the 1978 World Championships enjoyed as much encouragement from local fans as they could have expected if the meeting had been staged in London. Led by Robin Cousins and ice dancers Warren Maxwell and Janet Thompson, the team from the 'Old Country' was particularly close to Canadian hearts.

A surprising and respected cheerleader among scores of British supporters who made the journey was Vicki Wylde, sixteen, of Camberwell, who had contested the national Junior Championships but now hobbled on crutches after surviving multiple injuries in a London car crash.

Cousins, her idol and loyal friend, could hardly believe it when told of her arrival. 'That settles it,' he shouted delightedly. 'I've just got to win for her.' The British Champion had recovered well from a mild flu virus a fortnight earlier.

The men's event took pride of place because the issue looked wide open and the jumping seemed likely to be higher than ever. The same trio who had battled it out for the European contest only a month earlier were expected again to be the front runners, along with two Americans, Charles Tickner and David Santee, each with the known capability to run them close.

Cousins held fourth place after the figures, but stayed within reasonable range of Kovalev, the Russian defender, and Hoffmann, the European Champion. The unpredictable Kovalev held a small but precious advantage over Hoffmann at the end of the three figures and Tickner kept Cousins in fourth place. Kovalev narrowly led Hoffmann after the opening rocker figure, six of the nine judges opting for the Russian. Tickner and Santee were then third and fourth, each only fractionally ahead of Cousins.

In the second figure, the paragraph double three, Hoffmann had six judges marking him above Kovalev, but the Moscow skater stayed ahead by a whisker. Cousins improved, overhauling Santee for fourth position with a well-controlled tracing.

In the final figure, the change loop, Kovalev laid down the best tracings, gaining a firmer lead over the East German. Cousins also consolidated his margin above Santee. Having emerged from the figures with well-founded hopes of overhauling any of the leaders, the main concern for Cousins now was that his usually

Above: Presented to H.M. the Queen on March 29th, 1979, during a Royal Ice Gala at Wembley Arena, London, to mark the centenary of the National Skating Association of Great Britain

Above right: The moment of a lifetime – wearing the cherished Olympic gold medal and acknowledging the ovation after a memorable victory at Lake Placid on February 21st, 1980

Right: A dash of exuberance ends with a spray of ice flakes on the outdoor Plaza Ice Rink in Denver

Preparing for an exhibition, free from the worries of competition, complete with matching blue boot coverings

A stroll through downtown Denver between practice sessions at the Colorado Ice Arena

With tutors and fellow pupils at Denver. Standing, from left to right, Simone Grigorescu (U.S.A.), Scott Hamilton (U.S.A.), Carlo Fassi, Robin Cousins and Christa Fassi. Sitting, from left to right, Emi Watanabe (Japan), Kristina Wegelius (Finland), Susan Broman (Finland), and Claudia Binder (Austria)

Reaching new heights with obvious pleasure against a backdrop of Colorado Rockies

reliable stamina would not be unduly weakened through losing eleven pounds during his virus illness.

Hoffmann became the new leader when he passed Kovalev after the shorter of the two free skating sessions. Tickner remained third. Cousins was still fourth, but narrowed the gap between himself and the three above him – outpointing them all with a superior display of seven obligatory elements.

He would have done even better if his music had not been affected by a short-circuit in the sound system's volume control, thus disturbing his concentration. Despite this, three judges gave him 5·9 for presentation. He achieved a great double loop jump and brilliantly leapt double and triple toe loops.

Kovalev lacked spinning finesse, and dropped marks accordingly. A grandstand finish was now promised, with Hoffmann, who was next best to Cousins in the short free, looking difficult but still possible for the Briton to overhaul.

Just how Charles Tickner became the new World Champion in Ottawa, with Jan Hoffmann runner-up and Robin Cousins third, baffled many who followed the closest men's finish in living memory.

Cousins again proved to have no peer in free skating, out-jumping, out-spinning and out-scoring every opponent to gain a supplementary gold medal in this division. That he gained only a bronze medal for his overall performance seemed almost a travesty of justice, particularly considering the marks he must have forfeited when that earlier fault in the sound system had distorted his music.

The official score sheet confirmed that four of the nine judges placed Hoffmann first, three put Cousins in front, and only two voted for Tickner. Because the required majority of five judges failed to place either ahead, a collective majority of firsts and seconds decided the issue. This is how each judge placed the top three:

Judge	1	2	3	4	5	6	7	8	9	Majority
Charles Tickner	2	3	2	1	2	2	2	2	1	8 x 2 & 1
Jan Hoffmann	3	1	1	3	3	1	1	3	2	5 x 2 & 1
Robin Cousins	1	4	3	2	1	4	3	1	3	4 x 2 & 1

Only the French judge (number nine) placed the first three in the precise order they finished. It is a quirk of skating's complex majority-placings system that produced this rare tie-break. Surely a simpler method should be devised which could be more widely understood.

That Tickner deserved to win is not in question, but, in both the figures and free skating, the three were almost inseparable and one could easily feel for Hoffmann and Cousins. Incidentally, the three shared a healthy mutual respect for each other both on and off the ice.

Despite this enthralling cliff-hanger and the humbling of Kovalev, the fourth-placed Champion, the much less known Vern Taylor, of Canada, who finished only twelfth, almost overshadowed all else by achieving the first triple axel jump in competition, a mighty leap from a forward take-off involving three-and-a-half mid-air rotations.

Cousins landed three brilliant triples — loop, toe loop and salchow — and his only error was when two-footing a fourth, another toe loop. Eight judges gave him 5·9 for presentation, a score not received from any judge by either of the other medallists.

Before the 1978 World Championships in Ottawa, I had a very unpleasant virus infection and lost eleven pounds in weight. In consequence, I was unable to complete the full daily quota of training really required for a world championship until the last four or five days before departing for Ottawa.

On arrival, I seemed to pick up the competition spirit, which obviously helps with whatever one does, and that spirit can carry anyone through to the actual time of the event. The pre-championship practice went very well, much better than we had dared to hope, and, although at this late stage I had still not properly run through either of my free programmes, I was beginning to feel for the first time in three weeks that I was capable of making it.

The draw was favourable because we got the same group of figures as in Strasbourg and I knew that I was going to be able to correct faults that I had made there and maybe do better. So, despite the earlier setback, I felt in great spirits on the morning of the compulsory figures and proceeded to put down three tracings probably as good as, if not better than, any set I had done before.

A few of the judges acknowledged this and gave me very satisfying marks, while others gave me the kind of marks that I had been accustomed to receiving when less accurate. Still, a fourth place for figures in a World Championship was more than I had expected.

Already, I was ahead of two of the skaters who had been above me at the corresponding stage of the European event in Strasbourg, also the American, David Santee, whom I had never before beaten in the compulsories. I was therefore very happy with the situation, as was my professional, and we were thinking then that a bronze or even a silver were perhaps within my range.

The short programme was going to be my last performance of this particular arrangement, having used it for two seasons, and I was looking forward to giving it a good send-off. But, very unfortunately, the skater performing immediately before me, David Santee, experienced some fluctuations in his music and volume during the last ten or fifteen seconds of his programme.

I suffered similar distortions right from the very beginning of my programme. At times, the sound system seemed to have switched itself off completely, then, at others, came on so loud that it was impossible to hear any notes at all. I am positive that this distracted from my overall presentation. But I did complete everything I had to do so far as the technical content was concerned, and the

The British team putting our best feet forward at the Skaters' Ball in the London Hilton, following the 1977 National Championships – Alan Beckwith, Ruth Lindsey, me, Karena Richardson, Warren Maxwell and Janet Thompson

judges appeared to take this into consideration, although I know that I could probably have achieved better marks for the presentation side with the sound system working correctly. As it was, I finished second in this section to the East German, Jan Hoffmann.

It is important for skaters to have the music absolutely right during a competition, so the first thing I did when I had finished the short free was skate over to the referee and make sure that the tape recorder and/or sound system was corrected before the next skater came on.

It is only fair that everybody should get the best possible chance of doing well without having to worry about having music or ice problems beyond their control while they are competing.

Although second in the short programme, I was still fourth in the figures and short combined, and appreciated that I was going to have to go all out in the long programme if a medal were to be gained. Which colour it might be was anyone's guess because this was shaping up to a very, very close contest.

Each of the top five skaters was still well within range of a medal and there was every prospect of a very good finish. The first of these leaders to perform in the long free was Charlie Tickner, of the United States, who, so far as I could tell later from television and from listening to the audience at the time, skated just about the best performance of his career.

The judges appreciated this and gave him high marks. I then realized that, if I were really going to be in with a medal chance, I would have to do better than I had done in previous championships. Not having been able to finish in the previous year's event, I was going to have to prove myself all over again as a free skater on this side of the Atlantic, even though I had already been gold medallist in the free skating at Strasbourg.

As I went out there to start, I knew, too, that I was going to have to 'nurse' my stamina – remembering the loss of weight – to try and make sure I could get through the whole programme without flagging or making mistakes through tiredness.

Unfortunately, I committed a little error on one of the triples, but did manage to make it through the programme, and the rest went very well. I received a standing ovation and again came away with a gold medal for free skating and a bronze medal for the overall third placing – my first medals in a World Championship.

8
Touring and Reflecting

'If there were ever a contest for Mr Popularity among international figure skating stars, Robin Cousins could probably win hands down.' Thus wrote Linda Jade Stearns, when editor of *Canadian Skater*, after watching him infuse laughter into a busload of Skate Canada competitors.

Puzzled when she asked how he can look so calm during a competition, Robin smiled: 'You have to ignore the pressure; otherwise you get up tight.' Brother Martin marvelled: 'Robin just shrugs off tension. You never see him pacing up and down; he doesn't get irritable.'

Writing in the *Toronto Globe and Mail*, Nora McCabe echoed worldwide reactions of sports journalists:

'Cousins has those soft, fluid knees that make his stroking seductively silky. A crisp, powerful jumper with tremendous elevation that adds drama to his performance, he is also artistic with supple, expressive arm and torso movements.

'Perhaps his most impressive move is his flying sit spin, in which he folds his slender six foot frame so low it seems to skim the ice, then rises, clutching his free leg and pulling it over his head.

'Watching Cousins work out, one is struck by his dedication, determination and drive, qualities all world-class athletes share. On ice, he doesn't goof around.

'Off ice, Robin initially appears to be a typical teenager. His room looks like a cyclone hit it. Clothes are draped everywhere. The TV blares, any junk programme on the dial. Pleasant-looking, with neatly trimmed brown hair and deep blue eyes, he is popular with other skaters. Although turned twenty, he still giggles and does all the nutty things skaters do to relax and he still develops crushes on girls with the regularity of a student.

'However, talk to Cousins briefly and what emerges is an intelligent, thoughtful person who is meticulous about planning every bit of his career from costumes to choreography. For a skater, he is amazingly articulate.'

We left Ottawa directly after the World Championships there to take part in my first world tour – an annual series of exhibitions given by world championship medallists plus a few of the other most spectacular performers, specially organized by the International Skating Union.

Our first stop was Montreal, then on through Canada to Quebec City, Fredericton, Halifax, Toronto, Edmonton, Lethbridge and Vancouver. We were a little disappointed with the size of some of the Canadian audiences, though 5000 or 6000 people can look a smaller crowd than it really is in arenas big enough to hold more than twice that number. Even so, advance publicity apparently had not been as good as expected – unless it was just that Canadians had been swamped with skating on television.

We were not given too much time to look around and see what the cities were really like, but everywhere we went we were very well looked after and taken to eat at excellent restaurants.

Crossing to the States, we performed in Los Angeles, Oakland, Colorado Springs, Cleveland, Washington, Philadelphia and Providence. Particularly memorable was Los Angeles, where we had most enjoyable trips to Disneyland and the Universal film studios. We were rather scared when we found that we were going to perform before some 15,000 people at the Los Angeles Forum. Our show there was, for me at least, probably the best of the entire tour and resulted in a standing ovation.

Californians can be both critical and very appreciative and, happily, they seemed to enjoy especially the disco number that I had in my routine. In Washington, we had a visit to the White House and to the Jefferson and Lincoln memorials.

We were in New York on the day of the Oscar awards and a few of us managed to get to a party organized by Truman Capote and Andy Warhol, in recognition of the Oscars, at the famous Studio 54 Club. That made a great break from the skating. The tour had been pretty hard work; we had been on a very strict schedule and, of course, needed to keep ourselves very much in shape. To me, the skating on the tour was almost as important as competitions because most of the people had come to see world champions and medallists performing world-class programmes.

Our last stop was Providence, Rhode Island, and the show there was one of the most enjoyable – except for the fact that it was the last, and everyone would be going their separate ways the following day. It was one of the longest tours of its kind that had been organized. Three-and-a-half weeks is a long time and many of us had become so friendly with skaters from other countries and had such a good time together that we really did not want to leave. But equally, most of the skaters were worn out, so it made the parting easier.

In that finale at Providence, we managed to arrange, without the organizers knowing, what was probably the skating world's most experienced 'kick line.' Most professional ice shows incorporate with their chorus girls what they always call a kick line, which starts at one end of the rink with everyone doing swing

A graceful forward spiral

kicks. Well, we amateurs decided to emulate this and, led off by Sasha (Aleksandr) and Irina Zaitsev, Anett Pötzsch, Jan Hoffmann and Charlie Tickner, we all proceeded to make our own kick line, much to the audience's amazement – and ended up with probably the warmest reception of the whole tour. It was a fun end and, I think, a fitting one.

Are compulsory figures really on the way out? There have been rumours whirling about the skating world that they may soon disappear from senior international competition. Their removal is certainly under active discussion.

However, if figures are dropped from international senior championships, there must be some new system to ensure that an agreed standard of figures is reached by each skater before that skater be allowed to compete.

That is the crux of the matter. For more than thirty years, it has been constantly argued that figures are not what the general public want to see. Dick Button, the former Olympic and World Champion, once likened compulsory figures to an imaginary golf championship wherein part of the competition 'consisted merely of the usage of standard clubs chosen by lot – and everything done in triple repetition.'

The defence for keeping figures has always been that if skaters were not thus compelled to learn the basic technique which figures provide, the quality of free skating would deteriorate.

Figures elimination for seniors depends upon general agreement on a foolproof plan to safeguard required standards in figures. The answer may lie in a special ISU-sanctioned test which all competitors would be required to pass before entering a championship.

An internationally judged test would be needed, rather than the acceptance of existing national proficiency certificates, which lack uniformity. Only on such a condition would the abolition of figures from senior championships be agreeable to most member nations of the ISU. It should be stressed that it is not the need to practise figures which is currently in question, but only their continued inclusion in those events most dependent on spectator appeal.

There seems little likelihood, at present, of reaching agreement on any new method of calculating results considered as fair as the present one, yet simpler for the public to understand.

Under the existing system, total placements and aggregate marks are only of academic interest. Although normally they are a good indicator, neither total is in itself a deciding factor. Surely, no statistical results in sport are so confusing for the layman to follow as those in figure skating.

The only reasonable alternative international system appears to be one in which the majority-placings method be replaced by a combination of two conditions – the elimination of the two highest and two lowest marks (a principle adopted in diving and gymnastics) interlinked with a rotational substitution of judges so that no skater be marked by a compatriot.

Judging panels now frequently show puzzling discrepancy between their

Studiously tracing a compulsory figure

marking of the compulsory figures and the free skating. Why is the highest mark for figures often only around 4·5 out of six when 5·8 and more is frequently awarded for jumps and spins?

This apparently deliberate downgrading of the figures seems wholly unjustified and its continuance could invite an increasing disregard for the basic technique so essential to the preservation of good-quality skating, even though the overall result of an event may not be affected.

If everything possible is not done to ensure the maintenance of diligent training in figures, the general standard of free skating would gradually fall and the long-term outcome could be, as one eminent authority has suggested, 'a series of clowns cavorting about the rink.'

Figures are the basis of all skating, just as scales are the basis of piano playing and dressage the basis of show jumping. You cannot produce a good form of skating unless you understand the groundwork which figures teach.

If any proposal to drop figures from senior international championships eventually gains approval, as seems possible, on the grounds that figures are not 'flash' for spectators, I think it would be a very bad thing. I believe it should remain necessary for skaters to reach a specific standard in figures in order to be able to compete.

Should the ISU ever see fit to split up the competitions and have separate championships for the figures – they already award separate small medals for the figures section – perhaps this would be acceptable if these also acted as qualifying events for free skating championships. Personally, I believe the ideal thing would be to leave the format exactly as it is, thus obliging skaters to work harder at whichever is their weaker part of the event. As one whose figures used to be far more inferior to my free skating than they are now, I can speak with feeling and appreciation about this controversial situation.

Compulsory figures are always made to seem harder than they really are by the peculiarly high standard set by the judges in most competitions, whatever the grade. Consequently, the marks given for figures are always relatively low, when compared to those awarded in free skating.

When one reaches high standards in free skating, it should be offset by a wider margin of marks for the figures. Skaters are being tied down too often on marks for their figures simply because the judges do not use the full range of marks at their disposal. I have seen many a figure that has been worth a lot more marks than those awarded to a free skating programme.

Higher and more difficult jumps, underlined by the first triple axel in 1978, are the most spectacular general trend evident in recent World Championships.

This art has progressed remarkably since the American, Dick Button, achieved

82

the first-ever triple (loop) in 1952. Nowadays, at least five variations are accomplished in every international men's championship.

Any man would be scorned for failing to attempt one, and they are even commonplace among the top women; but amid the enthusiasm for such feats of athleticism it must be remembered that a skater is not (or should not be) marked for jumping merit alone.

Clearly a skater deserves more marks for a triple than a double, but it should not necessarily follow that the best jumper be top scorer in the free skating. Versatility is surely as important and more marks ought to be deducted for what is not included.

A return to a better general standard of all-round ability in free skating will come about only if competitors are more clearly penalized when either omitting specific spins or not performing them well.

Spinning has become a comparatively neglected skill and it is thus the more refreshing and encouraging to observe the exquisite finesse in this department displayed by Robin Cousins. The Bristol skater is now freely acknowledged as the world's best jumper, but he dominated the spinning by a far greater margin and his linking footwork is also unmatched.

Seeing the lighter side with coach Carlo Fassi

When I was first learning the basics of skating, I used to spend most of my time spinning like a top. I worked on my spins constantly because I loved doing them. The jumps I used to enjoy as well, except that I did not like falling over at the end. So I never used to work quite so hard on those.

Concentrating on figures was difficult at first, though in later years I enjoyed them very much because I understood them more and how much they contributed to technique. I think it is essential that youngsters are taught from the outset to appreciate that figures are the basics of skating. But it detracts from the enjoyment of doing figures if you have to get up very early in the morning to do them, as is so common in Britain because of the ice time problems.

I love to free skate and I thoroughly enjoyed jumping around from the beginning. But there was a time, as I started to work on double jumps, when problems arose because I was so skinny and bony that I used to get awful bruises and cuts. To counter this, I used to shove big, thick foam pads inside my trousers around the knees and ankles, to cushion the pain of the falls. It seemed to help a lot, because my confidence grew much more quickly from then on. But, in the early days, it was always the spins which would appeal to me most.

One of my advantages, especially in the short programme, is in spins and linking steps and footwork – and that was a particular benefit from learning with Pam. Whereas most of the coaches will concentrate on what is absolutely necessary, *i.e.* the jumps, some spins, some basic movements and the figures, Pam was always insistent about working extra hard on spins of all kinds and made me concentrate from the very beginning on making up my own footwork, because this was what other people were neglecting. It was, therefore, an advantage which all of her pupils have always had.

9
Music and Leisure

Music, I find, is becoming more important as the years go on, because the technical skating standard of competitions has now risen to such a level that contestants are having to search elsewhere for the extra points from the judges.

You need music which the audience is going to appreciate or instantly recognize. A skater may find a piece of music which he quite likes and, after hearing it several times more, may like it very much. But it must be remembered that the judges and spectators will hear that music only once and, hopefully, enjoy it at the first time of hearing. If they feel the urge to tap their feet or even clap to the beat, so much the better.

I like to vary the type of music I use, ranging from classics to films to instrumental rock or anything that is going to be different yet easily linked together and, at the same time, that will ring the changes of mood in a programme. Film music is generally very acceptable, but for competitions vocals are not allowed because, obviously, the words would distract from the performance.

The type of music which I prefer to use for skating is something that is nicely arranged. But you can find some music that will sound great in your living room and very good as you listen to it on a record-player, yet when you take it to the rink and play it over the public address system, it can sometimes get quite lost. A big arena has to take a big volume of music and, if you have a single instrument like a piano or violin, a really excellent recording is necessary, and even then you have to hope that the sound system in the rink will be good, too.

Stanley Black recordings are the ones that I frequently plumped for. I have used a lot of his music, mainly because his orchestrations are so readily adaptable for the ice – and they are usually suitably loud as well.

Black is very orientated to popular music with new arrangements. Most of the music I have used appears to have been well appreciated by audiences and judges alike. I think much more care could be taken by many skaters over their choice of music – and then their cutting (splicing and linking the tapes). I do not believe enough attention is paid to the quality of tapes and discs that are used now and am convinced that, with the standard of music rising all the time, it is vital to give proportionately more time to this aspect of programme preparation.

I will cite some examples to show the variation of music that I have used. One of my better pieces for a short programme was 'Perks' Theme' from the soundtrack of the film, *The Railway Children*. This was very happy-go-lucky and bouncy and something that the audience quickly went along with.

In complete contrast, the opening piece from my long programme in 1977 was from the title track of *El Dorado*, by the Electric Light Orchestra, a band which has become very popular both in Britain and America. They have produced some ideal music for skating competitions and exhibitions.

Michel le Grand wrote and recorded the music for the Diana Ross film, *Lady Sings the Blues*, which I incorporated in 1978 with some incidental music from the film, *Yellow Submarine*. Despite its contrasting style, it fitted well with the other pieces and changed the mood as required.

I always like to have pieces of music which are either very, very similar, so they will fit together without anyone noticing, or else obvious contrasts. Another piece I have enjoyed skating to was from the Mel Brooks' film, *Silent Movie*, which was a ragtime-cum-sleazy blues style, easy for interpretation.

One of the more enjoyable aspects of making up and taping routines is to be able to do it all yourself. In fact, I cut and tape all my own music and also choreograph my programmes. That way, you manage to express *your* true feelings, rather than someone else's.

Obviously, you cannot see yourself while performing, so Carlo and his wife, Christa, say if they do not think something is being put to its best advantage in one particular part of the rink. Guided by constructive comment, one can change around something so that, for example, it can be seen to better advantage by the judges.

But aside from such improvements, the basic choreography, the movements and the elements I place in the programme myself, and alter them until everything seems satisfactory.

To me, skating is all about being able to get on to the ice and express my feelings to an audience through music and through the movements that make up skating – the jumps, the spins, and the steps. I do not think you can differentiate between skating as a sport and as an art, because the idea is to make the sport like an art. On the ice I have never felt insecure. I have never gone out on the ice and thought I should not be here. I enjoy every second of it.

I like to make an audience happy with my skating. When they clap in time and I can hear their oohs and ahs, it gives an uplift to my skating.

The idea of the first few bars of music is basically to attract attention. Al-

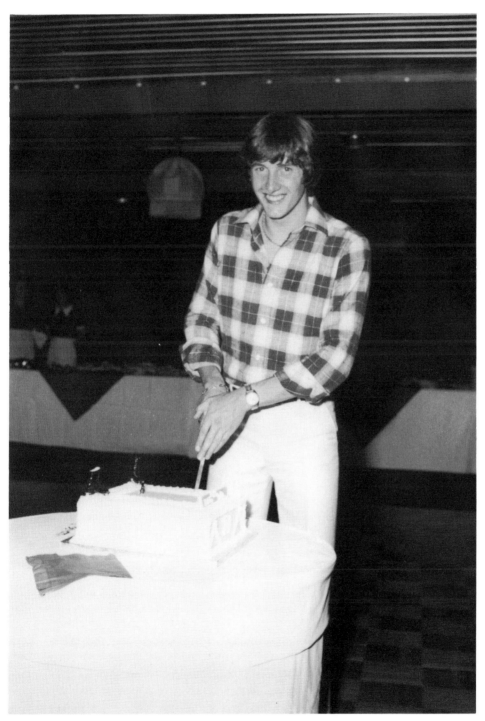

Cutting the cake at my 21st birthday party in Bristol

though you have already been announced, a lot of people are probably still talking and even some of the judges are looking at their notes, so for me a big opening – whether the skater is moving or not – is important to make sure that everybody is focussed on you.

Normally, skaters will put their programmes together and have the jumps as their main assets, then use easy steps and little pieces in between to link them together. What I try and aim for, so far as is possible, is to have the steps and the programme itself as the main body, making the jumps incidental so that it looks less obvious that I have done so much preparation for them.

When I make up new programmes, I never write down what I do. I have this habit of finding an empty evening at the ice rink, putting on the music over and over again and just improvising each time to it – and I go on and on until those improvisations become regular routine.

For the Lake Placid Olympics, I chose music with a slow opening because I liked to think that my skating that season would be as easy-looking and about as perfect as I could make it. I intermixed it with some rather update, Spanish-style music, to contrast not only with the style of the other music used but also my style of skating. It was very heavily orchestrated, allowing plenty of scope for jumps and spins and skating very fast, which the audience seemed specially to like.

Having said all this, when you are competing there is no set. There is nothing but you and the ice – and you really have to make good use of that.

Exhibitions are a big outlet for championship skaters, especially if they happen to come soon after a competitive period has ended. It is a time when skaters can relax and just go out and enjoy themselves as much as the audience enjoys watching. They can let their hair down and perform in whatever way they feel.

Many exhibitions are really as much for the benefit of the skaters as for the onlookers because the skaters are given free reign to present what they please. Pair skaters and ice dancers welcome the opportunity to include moves of a kind not permitted in their respective competitions and soloists will sometimes include handstands, cartwheels and even back somersaults – exhibition-type moves not normally seen in championships. The crowds love it and, for the performers, a change is as good as a rest.

The more successful and higher ranking you become, the more exhibitions you get asked to do and I have travelled in many countries as an amateur, guesting in skating galas, some of them helping worthwhile charities.

Since being in the States, I have found that many shows put on by local amateur clubs have been up to professional standards, not only in skating ability, but in quality of big production numbers and costumes.

It brings all the hard work from competitions to a happy climax when you get invited to perform in such shows and exhibitions. You get presents and various social invitations, the audiences get pleasure from watching you and, as an amateur, you feel good to think that people have paid and are having a good time while you are also enjoying yourself by doing just whatever you feel like doing.

One of the charity ice galas that I appeared in at Queen's Ice Club in London was attended by Princess Margaret, to whom a cheque was presented on behalf of the skaters. Comedian Ronnie Corbett was a guest at the dinner which followed and we even managed to persuade him to put on a pair of skates and be taken around the ice.

On another occasion, at Solihull in aid of the Muscular Dystrophy Association we were honoured by the presence of Jane Seymour, the actress, and we managed to get her on skates, too. She even accepted our invitation to meet us later at another rink to try a further spell of skating during a public session.

Meeting celebrities is one of the perks for exhibition skaters. During the 1978 world tour, Neil Diamond's backing group came to see us at the Los Angeles Forum. In 1976, Elton John gave a big concert at Earls Court, London, for the British Olympic Association, and some of us who had given exhibitions to assist the Olympic funds were invited and able to meet Elton afterwards at a reception.

My own attempts at show business off the ice haven't always been successful. I was once called upon by a television station (HTV) to present a series of six children's programmes to give information on events of the week and local topics. During one such programme, we featured three Afghan hounds and, as I was interviewing their owner, one of them – sitting on a huge box next to me – insisted on turning his head away from the camera and exposing his rear quarters instead.

Three Afghan hounds with all the studio lighting on their fur are bound to be hot, and their panting was coming over the air louder than our talking. When the one on the box saw something on the other side of the room that he liked the look of, he leapt off the box and took me with him – in mid-conversation. Yes, I understand what people mean who advise you not to compete with animals in show business.

Not only have I always done my own choreography and tapes, but also the design for my costumes, which my mother has then made. I always like to keep costumes simple and clean-looking with nice lines, so that the outfit itself does not distract from the skating.

Frequently, you will find a skater's clothes covered in glitter and sequins. If you are forever looking at the off-the-shoulder cut or the low front or the gaudy colours being worn, attention tends to be diverted from the music and the skating.

I try and keep to straightforward colours that will match easily and can be trimmed neatly without getting to look like a Christmas tree. My costumes have been usually very basic and plain and only during the past year or two have I sought outside help in getting materials dyed and trimmed.

I am thankful to my mother for all the hard work she has done for me by pattern-cutting my costumes. It is very time-consuming, but at least my Mum sees her creations as well as her son on the television.

One of the really enjoyable aspects of ice skating is the excitement it generates in the very young. Naturally, I know and give encouragement to many of them.

Peter Fuidge, when a seven-year-old Bristol skater, invaded our house one day with some contemporaries while his mother called to collect something. Little Peter looked up at his Mum and asked: 'Does Robin live here?'

Assured that I did, he looked around with a puzzled expression before commenting: 'I always thought he lived in a castle.' For some reason, he had nurtured this idea that I had some kind of regal status and I just hope he was not too disappointed.

Another young Bristol skater, Emma Erentz, who was only four at the time, was watching me on television one day and suddenly started crawling around the back of the set. When asked what she was doing, it transpired that she was trying to take the back off so that she could get inside and skate with me, like she did on Sunday mornings in public sessions.

Needless to say, there have been plenty of humorous interludes during my skating travels. During an exhibition tour of England's Silver Blades rinks in 1975, a group of leading skaters of the day were taken to Paddington station from our hotel in London's West End in three chauffer-driven limousines, complete with pennants.

The party included the Americans, Dorothy Hamill and her mother, Canadians Ronnie Shaver and Lynn Nightingale, Britain's Janet Thompson with Warren Maxwell and the Hungarian ice dancers, Krisztina Regoeczy and Andras Sallay. As we drove past gawping onlookers at Paddington, Mrs Hamill began to give the royal wave as everyone was most interested to see who these important people were arriving in such state, only to observe the chauffeurs opening the doors and letting out a group of young 'anybodies' dressed in jeans and T-shirts and, except for the elegant Mrs Hamill, looking about as scruffy as we could be, as was often our wont when travelling between galas.

Many hotels abroad have coke or other soft drink machines installed on each floor. One very late night or early morning after the 1977 World Championships had ended in Tokyo, someone had managed to unplug one of these machines and place it very neatly in the centre of the floor of the lift at the Keio Plaza Hotel, where we were all staying. It was quite remarkable to see how guests reacted after pressing the lift button and, when the doors opened, finding themselves confronted by a coke machine. Some failed to remain inscrutable and others, equally surprisingly, inserted coins in the machine.

On various hotel floors during other championships, fire extinguishers have been known to go off for no apparent reason and have literally soaked various people – even delegates of the International Skating Union if they happened to come out of the lift at the wrong time. But these are fairly harmless pranks that young skaters are apt to get up to and, I suppose, any athletes would get up to, just to let off their safety valves at the end of tense competitions.

I am not very superstitious, although I never walk under a ladder. I do not carry a special good luck charm, but I do have sellotaped to my skate-bag a natural four-leaf clover which a lady fan gave me at the 1976 Innsbruck Olympics. She also gave one each to John Curry and Dorothy Hamill at the same time. I just carry that around with me as a memento.

At various competitions I am given little good luck charms by various well-wishers, but there is nothing that I feel I have to have with me. If you did develop such a habit and should one day forget what you think brings you luck, then psychologically you could fret about it and your performance could suffer.

Lots of the girls do have little charms which they pin to the inside of a sleeve or other part of the dress. The American, Linda Fratianne, was noted for that. She had her own little bag of good luck seeds – heather, I believe – pinned in her dress every time she skated. Fluffy animal mascots are also frequently to be seen left beside a girl's skate-bag while she is performing.

I try not to be superstitious about such things as picking number thirteen – when I have, it has often brought me good luck – and I do not mind wearing green, but know many who do mind.

Although you can hardly call it a superstition, I never clean my skates on the day of a championship. It is always done well in advance. I usually clean them a little before an event is due and often do not do so again until the next contest looms up. It is just a habit.

A question I am frequently asked is whether much friction goes on between rival skaters at championships; whether we really do get along well together or merely make out that we do for the sake of appearances.

My answer is that if you were to come to the competitors' hotel, to the restaurant where all the skaters eat, you would not find us at separate tables. More than likely, all who are able to converse together in the same language will be sitting together, regardless of nationality, probably discussing their plans for whatever social functions have been arranged.

A lot of skaters from different countries train together, particularly in America, where some coaching schools enjoy a very cosmopolitan attendance. In Denver, where I have trained, there were seldom fewer than eight international competitors preparing at the same time. Many rivals from different nations train under the same coach at the same rink and there are frequent

I become British Champion in 1976 – and the demand for autographs threatens
to exceed supply

examples of this in big cities like London and Toronto, so for many of us there is not much adjusting to do after arriving at a championship venue.

Eastern European skaters are as friendly as they are allowed to be. I say that because there are times when their officials tend to segregate them more than others. But in the dressing rooms and during exhibition tours, we all get on very well together.

At the beginning of each new season, you meet everybody again and find out what has been happening during the months between. Then, as the new season progresses, everyone seems to get close again like one big happy family, and, by the time the last meeting ends, the girls sometimes even cry about having to go home and not being able to see each other for a while. It all gets quite emotional and this is a great thing in skating, apparently quite different from some sports in which, so I gather, it can sometimes get very nail-biting and quite bitchy between participants. Of course, one can only generalize and those who look hard enough can, I suppose, always find the odd exception.

Broadly speaking, competitors in most winter sports get on extremely well together during the Olympics and it is difficult to understand why, when national representatives in one field can obviously enjoy such harmony, the world at large can be in such a mess.

10
All Worthwhile

Of all the rivals I have striven to beat, the most important to me was John Curry. In the days when we were in opposition, I never really thought of myself as being able to beat him, but always regarded him as someone to look up to. I aimed for the same standard that he was setting at the time.

Even so, it didn't come as a great shock to me when I did so nearly defeat him that last year we met in our national championships. Whether or not that in itself had any effect on him, or gave him some kind of boost to do better in the internationals which followed and so go on to win his three titles, is something we shall never know for sure, but it is nice to reflect that perhaps I was in some way instrumental in his ultimate glory.

Although I never really considered myself a threat to John, it was good to be able to use him as a gauge for my improvement – to come back each year to the British Championships and see how much closer I had drawn to John's level. When he retired, I resolved to strive for an Olympic gold medal and follow the example of his preparation, his temperament during competition and his attack – the way that he geared himself through the three days of a championship. I hoped to be able to use a lot of the tips that I learned from watching John train and compete, to help me on my way up.

Another opponent I admired was Jan Hoffmann. He had tremendous technical ability, but, typical of so many East European skaters, tended to skate very much as instructed – and this can lead to the mechanical, robot-like style which so many of them appear to have.

Jan's ability to lay down good compulsory figures was always a great advantage. Indeed, he was a consistently strong all-rounder. It was most unfortunate that, at a very important time in his career – immediately after he had won both European and World titles – he had cartilage trouble.

Unlike my own troubles in that area, either the diagnosis was made very late or the operation was not as successful as expected, so he was obliged to miss a complete season of competition. In subsequent seasons, he had a great struggle to regain his earlier form and eventually recapture the titles.

Vladimir Kovalev is a Russian with a Russian temperament: a zany character off the ice as well as on it sometimes, and a lot of people really did not know how to take this guy. I didn't enjoy watching him skate, probably because I never knew what he was going to do next, and I like to be relaxed when I watch someone skate.

I could not try to compare Vladimir with John or Jan. He always had his own sense of character on the ice and one that really did not appeal to me.

Charlie Tickner was one of my closest rivals for quite a while. We each competed in our first international at the same time, in France at St Gervais, and have been very close rivals, beating each other on and off ever since. But that fact never changed a very good relationship between us off the ice.

I have always enjoyed Charlie's skating, a very individual style with a happy-go-lucky vein reminiscent of Ronnie Shaver. Each did his own thing, interpreting the music in an original way without trying to copy or introduce anybody else's style or movements. Charlie even invented a few of his own unique moves, which obviously helped him along to the 1978 World title.

I was a great admirer of the skating of John Curry and Toller Cranston, appreciating the very creative styles that each had. Toller was very abstract and would use the music to express feeling and emotion through his skating, whereas John was very poetic on the ice and would tend almost to weave a spell over the audience and take them in.

It is very difficult to compare the two because they were so different, even though each was striving for the same ultimate goal. It was a pity in a way that both were around at the same time. I think both were worthy of more than they achieved and, although John eventually did get recognition for his work and his art, it came one or two years too late for him to be able to improve further and get over to the people – the audiences and judges alike – what he would have liked to have been able to 'say' to them.

I cannot really compare myself with either John or Toller. I like to do my own type of skating. I do not style myself in one particular vein every time I make up a new programme or routine. I have done everything from classical ballet to disco jazz and, in my performances, like to do variations and change the mood – not too frequently, as that tends to distort my idea of the overall impression – but try and vary my routines each year, so that I do not become known as a skater who performs always in the same style or uses the same kind of music. I always hoped that the particular feeling I have could be used to advantage over others and that the judges would appreciate what it was that I was trying to do.

One of my idols has been the great Russian pair skater, Irina Rodnina, and not only her, but also her husband and partner, 'Sasha' Zaitsev. It was tremendous being able to spend three weeks with them, watching them during the 1978 world tour and seeing how they coped with what was, to them, an easy task after all the work they had done over the previous ten years for her and six years for them together.

The most incredible female skater I have seen – fast, very bold and almost masculine in her style, but still feminine enough to produce beautiful lines and emotion through her skating – that sums up Irina, a remarkable woman and without doubt one of the world's greatest skaters.

The ice dancer, Irina Moiseeva, is another Russian I could watch skate day in and day out, mainly for her interpretation and her ability to feel every single note of music, whether it be vocal or instrumental. She and her husband, Andrei Minenkov, take over the whole arena when they step on to the ice to perform. There is very much a commanding presence in Irina which impels you to watch everything she does; to marvel at the way she uses her eyes, and her every other means of self-expression.

Very rarely will you hear much applause during their performance, but you can always tell how much the crowd appreciates them at the end. It is curious because, when you are performing you love to hear a crowd, but people will get so involved in what such skaters are doing and trying to say, that they will in fact forget to applaud until the very end. Then, the crowd will suddenly break the atmosphere into a million pieces with thunderous applause, perhaps even a standing ovation.

This is something that some Russians have that a lot of the other skaters do not have, and that is an ability to command the audience's attention and to make onlookers appreciate what they are doing. Of course, John was able to do this too.

It always appears that, in the eyes of judges, a skater has to work his or her way up the ladder to achieve international recognition. One example of this would be Lisa Allen, of the United States, who competed in her first World Championship in Ottawa in 1978 and, in my opinion, presented the best free skating performances, both short and long, by a considerable margin.

Her only reward was to be placed fifth in the short and fourth in the long. Due to her relatively low figure placing – a situation which has a familiar ring to the writer – she was having to struggle in her free skating performances to gain due recognition. Had she been in, maybe, her third year of world competition, I am sure the result would have been very different. Fortunately for her, she still had a very good career ahead.

Skating is a very expensive sport at championship level and, if this be your goal, you have to be prepared to sacrifice an awful lot. The training requirements are very stiff and, in England, it is necessary to get up very early in the morning, probably having had to walk to the rink, and then practise for two or three

Charlie Tickner, the 1978 World victor in Ottawa and for years my major opponent

hours in the cold – and in the winter it is very damp too.

There are a lot of let-downs before the rewards begin, including test and competition disappointments. If you are going to be a champion, or at least aim to be, then you have to be prepared to work extra, extra hard. If you are not prepared to sacrifice a lot of things and most of your spare time, then my advice is either to forget the sport or, if you are going to skate, just do so for recreational pleasure.

Striving towards and maintaining championship standards entails parental backing and it is a big waste of their money when a young skater decides, 'Ah, this is getting too hard. I've had enough. I'm going to give up.'

With skating still regarded as a minority sport by sports councils and the like, the financial backing which ought to be available is not. I hope earnestly that, within the next few years, skating will be brought alongside the status of swimming and athletics, where it belongs, and that skaters may thus get a much better chance to train abroad if need be to attain the top standard, and generally be given more financial assistance for their coaching. Only in this way can they reasonably hope to compete on level terms with opponents from other nations.

The need to train abroad, so far as British skaters are concerned, should be only temporary. If sufficient money to help skating is forthcoming, more rinks should bring sufficient international facilities nearer home.

At the end of an amateur career and on the threshold of a professional one, I am asked whether I would do it again. Without hesitation, the answer is yes. I can never look back on all that I went through without recalling some bad times and even some times when I wished that I could have stopped.

But on the other side of the coin are all the perks that come with success, and the fact that you are able to visit foreign countries and be looked after like a VIP regardless of where you place in a competition. You have a tremendous advantage over a lot of other people who seldom even leave their own home town.

It was hard and it has been a big struggle, but the ultimate contests have been amply rewarding for all the work put in and all that my parents contributed, both in time and money, to help me along my way.

Among many people I am grateful to for helping my career, apart from my own family, are my sponsors in the latter competitive years, the Millers building company – thanks to Iris (*née* Lloyd-Webb), herself a successful former skater, and her husband. Much gratitude is due also to the Bristol Skaters' Supporters Club, which was originally formed solely for my benefit by Les Bradby, and I

Soviet pair skaters Sasha Zaitzev and Irina Rodnina demonstrating perfect control during a twist lift

Jan Hoffmann, my main rival in 1980, whose world championship victory in Dortmund thwarted my triple crown aspiration.

should like to thank him and his wife, Bet, and everyone else involved at the Bristol rink, not forgetting the club chairman, Jeff Williams, and his wife, Connie, and rink manager Bert Sale for making ice available to me, particularly at extra times when specially needed.

I appreciate, too, the schools and local organizations in and around Bristol which raised donations to help pay for various equipment, as did loyal individuals. All this was an immeasurable help and gave my career a tremendous spur.

Probably my main interest, apart from skating, is my drawing. This has stemmed from my school training in art. My favourite subjects at school were art, design craft and, at junior school, pottery. Rather than straightforward drawing of landscapes or portraits, I would much rather create my own characters or cartoons – an abstract type of work.

I have spent a lot of time doodling between competitions or when sitting in a hotel room with little else to do. A lot of my more complex drawings began as doodles and subsequently grew.

I can never sit down and listen to music without attempting to relate it to skating. Most pieces of music I listen to with a view to their possible use for skating, and I find that good classical music is often suitable. My taste in music ranges from classics to some contemporary rock right through to disco and 'funky' music. Going to discos has probably been one of my great outlets when skating abroad.

Skaters are usually good dancers and, after competitions, we frequently used to go and 'take over' a dance floor, usually in parties of twenty or more.

Other sports that I like are swimming and tennis. So far as tennis is concerned, perhaps I should qualify this by saying that I enjoy patting the ball and getting it over the net rather than that I am much of a player. My swimming ability was, I suppose, to some extent naturally inherited from my mother. Swimming in an outdoor pool in the sunshine certainly makes an agreeable change from enclosed skating rinks.

So I have managed to keep myself occupied when not skating, these other interests serving as relaxation, and thereby helping my skating career.

Skating for me has, or will have, a lot more to it than just working as an amateur and doing competitions. It has been my goal afterwards to join one of the big theatrical skating companies in a professional touring show, thus seeing more of the world and, hopefully, giving a lot more people pleasure from what I enjoy doing.

If I do well and get suitable parts in such shows, I could only skate in them for as long as it is possible to maintain my standard. Once I felt I had drained myself of my best skating ability – finding myself being less adventurous, taking bits out of the programme and consciously making it physically easier than when first joining the shows – I think that would be the time to get out of the public eye.

But, even after that, I know that I should still wish to stay involved in such shows, probably in choreography and production. I have enjoyed costume design and production work with amateur club shows in Bristol and would love to become more involved in that line, perhaps before eventually embarking on a coaching career.

11
Living in the States

During my brief stay at home after the 1978 World Championships in Ottawa, I was able to take a welcome rest – and a bit of a busman's holiday. My first public engagement while in England was what had become an annual trip to Birmingham, to Solihull Ice Rink to take part in the Muscular Dystrophy Gala, run every year by Peter and Nancy Andrews. Each year they have a celebrity to open the show and this time it was Simon Williams, who was one of the stars of the television serial, *Upstairs, Downstairs*. We had a super evening and a lot of money was raised for the charity.

I also made my first trip to one of the new sports complexes, the Magnum Ice Rink in the Irvine Sports Centre near Ayr, Scotland. Although there is a very enthusiastic young club membership there, I feel very sorry for them and others like them around the country who are using these sports centres, because such rinks are not big enough for serious skating. They are nowhere near international size.

In fact, Britain has very few international-sized rinks and I feel very strongly that a lot of money is wasted on some of the newer sports centres which have a small ice rink, a small gymnasium and a small swimming pool, none of which can be used for proper competitions. The pool is not long enough for an international championship and the rink is not big enough to hold a national championship, so after a while I think some of these multisports complexes are going to find themselves inadequate for all future needs. Everyone seems to appreciate such errors only after the damage has been done. It is usually too late afterwards to change things and too expensive to make a small rink larger.

What Britain badly needs is a very large sports centre in the middle of the country, equally accessible to all, with a pool long enough for swimmers to train properly and have national competitions and with a rink adequate to stage national and even international championships. The lack of facilities like this is initially off-putting for potential British champions. In this respect, I feel certain we are not doing as well as we are capable of doing.

I returned to Denver at the beginning of May, 1978, via Cleveland, Ohio, to skate in four days of exhibitions at the Cleveland Skating Club. This was my first visit to Cleveland and one of the most enjoyable shows in which I have participated.

The beginning of my training sessions for the new season at Denver's Colorado Ice Arena were taken up with learning new triples. We spent a lot of time doing the basic triples that I had been performing for a while, but I started working also on the triple lutz, triple flip and triple axel – the latter coming quite easily to me after a month or so. Although I was skating well and these jumps were not too bad, I have a feeling that practising them caused my injury – yes, another one.

It became apparent during a September session at the North American Training Camp in Lake Placid. This is run each year by Carlo Fassi in association with various professionals from Canada and the United States, a week-long seminar which involves many, many skaters being on the ice and just working with the professionals on different techniques of jumping and spinning. It was during this week that I started to feel soreness in my left leg. The seminar was good fun, although I think there were too many skaters on the ice for me to be able to do a lot of work. But it was most interesting to observe how other professionals teach and how some of the other skaters train.

After returning from the seminar, I spent time with various doctors in Denver to find out what the problem was. With a bone scan, they concluded that it was a stress fracture on the left shin brought on by the type of jumps I was doing, and just bad enough for me to be in pain when I was skating. It had been developing over quite a while. So I was advised to take a six-week rest, to clear up the problem.

I reflected later that, although the triple axel and the triple lutz had gone fine during the summer, these tremendous jumps probably did cause this injury, which kept me out of the Rotary Watches Ice International. But I was not upset at having to take the rest. It had been almost twelve months since I had had any holiday and this enforced one seemed to do me good because, although off the ice for six weeks, the minute I returned I felt very refreshed and new. I think this showed in the performances of the season to come.

The Wylies in Denver are one terrific family and I was very fortunate to be accepted into their home. Originally, it was just a temporary arrangement, but after a couple of weeks it turned into a couple of months and, eventually, a couple of years. Bob and 'B.L.,' Claire, Paul and Dawn have all played a very big part in my life in America. They are very much a family in which the family comes first, which to me is almost like being at home.

Mr Wylie is a geophysicist and works for Petroleum Information in Denver and Dallas. Mrs Wylie's connection with the rink is that she runs the skate shop

The man from the CIA – Colorado Ice Arena in this case – adjusting my laces in the stands

– the skatique as we call it – and both she and her husband have been very active skaters. Originally from Dallas, in Texas, the whole family is very skating-orientated. The daughters Dawn and Claire were aged nineteen and eighteen respectively and son Paul fifteen during my last year with them. The family have had skaters living in with them for most of their time in Denver.

I was first introduced to the Wylies by Cindy Perpich, a United States national skater from Chicago, who has trained with Carlo and Christa. Thanks to the Wylies, I have had no problems on or off the ice. They have spent much of their time doing for me exactly what they do for their own children and what my own parents would do, so I am naturally very grateful to them for all the help they have given me. I do not think my staying in America could have been nearly so good if it had not been for their kindness.

Living in the States is totally different from living in England. I think it is very difficult to compare the two life styles. In America, everything seems to me so free and easy. Living in Denver is different, largely because of the weather. In the evenings and at weekends, the Wylies and I tended to do things together as much as possible. In the summer, we spent a lot of time swimming, going to the mountains and enjoying other outdoor activities, whereas in England the weather generally doesn't allow anything much more adventurous than touring the shops.

Because of the September injury, my main worry at the time was whether or not I would be able to compete in the Rotary Watches Ice International, which was to be held during October in Richmond and would be the first international meeting of its type in my home country. Rotary Watches had done a lot in organizing this new venture, involving skaters from Czechoslovakia, France, Japan, the United States, the USSR and West Germany as well as Great Britain.

I was really looking forward to competing and using this as one of my stepping stones for the forthcoming World and European Championships, when I was told that I would have to withdraw. It was with great reluctance that I picked up the telephone to inform my parents. The organizers were upset to hear the news, but paid for my trip to England so that I could be at Richmond during the events and be on hand to help out in any way I could. So, although I hated sitting on the sidelines, I was still able to claim to be a part of the first Rotary Watches Ice International at Richmond, hopefully the first of very many of this type of competition to be held in Britain.

As Cousins moved relentlessly towards his third national title, at Richmond in late November 1978, his supporters were doubly reassured, first by his much more confident figures than during the previous season, and later by powerful jumps and fast spins, to dispel any lingering doubts about a knee beginning to rank in sporting fame with that of cricketer Denis Compton. He was apparently well recovered from the stress fracture that had caused him to miss the first Rotary Watches Ice International, held on the same rink the previous month.

Anxious to show compatriots how much his figures had improved during training in the United States, Robin did just that with some immaculate tracings and with better style than before. Andrew Bestwick was a non-starter owing to a foot injury and his non-appearance presented the title defender with an even easier task than was anticipated.

The absence of Bestwick was, in one sense, no help to the champion. At least

Spring in the air, 1978, celebrating the announcement of the new Rotary Watches Ice International to be held the following October. Kay Barsdell with Ken Foster (left), Alan Beckwith with Ruth Lindsey (centre) and Warren Maxwell with Janet Thompson

the Blackpool skater, if fit, would have been able to press Cousins enough to prompt a keener sense of urgency. The fact that Cousins was clearly in a national class of his own contrasted starkly with the final seasons of his illustrious predecessor.

That Cousins so very nearly defeated John Curry only a few weeks before Curry's historic triple crown achievement in 1976 meant that Curry must then have gained from their domestic duels. Cousins, in the 1978 British Championships, enjoyed no such advantage. It is difficult in any sport to attain peak form without pressure from one's adversaries. Fortunately, this seemed unlikely to affect Cousins unduly, for he is a man whose target has always been to improve on his previous personal best, irrespective of the opposition.

In that, he has succeeded remarkably well, at the same time brushing aside injury setbacks sufficient to sap the zeal of most mortals.

I was anxious when I first got back on to the ice to make sure that I would be fit and in good condition in time to return to England in November, 1978, to defend my British title. I remember there was some speculation as to whether I would be fit enough to perform at the standard for which I was hoping.

I arrived in London ready to go, and the practice sessions went exceptionally well. I was also helped by the fact that Christa Fassi was accompanying me for the first time at a British Championship – to be sure that everything was as Carlo had wished and to make sure that I would do everything they wanted me to do during the championship.

I was very pleased with the compulsory figures. I did not do a very good loop, but I feel that the other figures I put down, the rocker and the bracket, were two of the best I had done in competition – and this was reflected in some of the marks. I was a little disappointed with the short programme, basically because for me it is very difficult to skate without an audience (it was held in the afternoon). One of the little jokes of the day was that there were more competitors than spectators.

For the first time in my life, I was as freezing cold when I came off the ice as I had been when I went on, and I think this showed a little in the performance. I did everything as well as I could, but the absence of any sizeable audience caused me to have very little sparkle that day. However, few of the judges appeared to notice this and I had a good lead going into the long programme.

The following day, people were curious to see my new long programme, to see how fit I was and, no doubt, to compare me with the leading overseas entrants they had seen in the Rotary Watches Ice International on the same rink only a few weeks previously. I was beginning to feel a little bit of pressure, but, with the support that I had from my home club and from other rinks represented that night at Richmond, I feel I did a good job.

Working with my dance trainer, Darlene Garlutzo

I enjoyed skating in this championship. It was hard because I didn't know how well I was going to do so soon after the injury, but the outcome was personally satisfactory and I was feeling very happy and very eager to go on to Zagreb and Vienna for the two international championships.

One problem for me during the British event was that both my short and long programmes had to be altered at the last moment because of the judges sitting on chairs on the ice. I had been informed previously that this was going to be the first year when the judges would be sitting behind the barrier, leaving the whole of the ice surface for the skaters to use.

When you are accustomed to training on a rink bigger than the one at Richmond and it is belatedly decided to have the judges on the ice, it makes a lot of difference where you can go, and I found myself once or twice thinking that I might end up in one of the judges' laps. So we changed both programmes accordingly and, although it probably made no difference to the overall effect in the end, I feel that such adjustments should be unnecessary.

12
Que Será, Será

A main talking point on the eve of the 1979 European Championships in Zagreb, Yugoslavia, was not whether Robin Cousins could win a medal, but what its colour would be. Such was the confident form that he had been displaying. The general feeling was that he could certainly improve on the previous season's bronze. How Cousins himself felt was well known. 'My prime target is Olympic gold next season,' he said. 'Whatever may be collected on the way will be regarded as a bonus.'

In the event, he endured mixed fortunes. After the three compulsory figures, the Bristol skater held sixth position without allowing any of the tightly-bunched front-runners to draw far ahead. Vladimir Kovalev, the 1977 World Champion, was the overnight leader, with Jan Hoffmann, the East German defender, barely separable in second place. The next four, Igor Bobrin (USSR), Mario Liebers (East Germany), Jean-Christophe Simond (France) and Cousins were all within seven-tenths of a point of each other.

Cousins made a promising start in the opening rocker figure, scoring fourth-highest marks. Hoffmann led at this stage, pursued by Kovalev and Bobrin. It was the middle figure, the paragraph bracket, which tested Cousins' nerve the most. The tracing etched on the ice was below his best and he knew it had been tackled too slowly.

The British judge, Sally-Anne Stapleford, gave him the lowest marks among a panel of nine dominated by East Europeans, but Cousins, sportsman as always, responded: 'She was the only one right. It was a bad figure.' Hoffmann, despite illegally aligning both his circles with a blue line across the ice – used for ice hockey – got away with it and the top four stayed in the same order.

The final figure, the paragraph loop, produced a curious anti-climax. Hoffmann, Kovalev and Cousins each erred at this point, while Liebers and Simond excelled. But the real issue appeared still to rest between the previous year's three medallists – Hoffmann, Kovalev and Cousins.

Cousins improved his prospects the following day by convincingly winning the short free skating, soaring to third behind Hoffmann, the new leader, and Kovalev. With clearly the best performance of the day, Cousins skilfully combined double toe salchow and triple toe loop jumps in a display that was also rich in quality and versatility of spins. He earned a maximum six mark for presentation from the West

111

German judge. Kovalev and Hoffmann each also included a triple toe loop jump and survived without a major error, so Cousins faced no easy task to overhaul either or both in a likely close finish.

In a tense final session before an excited Zagreb crowd, the long free skating also belonged to Cousins, who included three triples – loop, toe loop and salchow – in a performance that received two more sixes for presentation. What a joy it was to see this man soar through the air. As in the previous season, he had the satisfaction of winning the supplementary gold medal for easily the best free skating perform-ance, but the overall title was successfully defended by Hoffmann, with Kovalev runner-up.

The result, as with the 1978 World Championships in Ottawa, was about the nearest one can get to a triple tie in figure skating. Four of the nine judges placed Hoffmann first, three chose Cousins (the overall top scorer) and the other two selected Kovalev. Because no one had a majority of firsts, the three had to be assessed on a collective majority of firsts and seconds. Thus, Hoffmann and Kovalev each had six firsts or seconds and Cousins five. The decision went to Hoffmann because he received four firsts, two more than Kovalev. Such a complex situation only arises, thank goodness, when skaters are abnormally close. For the record, the nine judges placed the top three thus:

Judge	A	B	C	D	E	F	G	H	I	Total placements	Total points
Hoffmann	3	1	3	1	1	2	1	4	2	18	184·04
Kovalev	1	2	2	3	2	1	2	3	4	20	183·98
Cousins	2	3	1	2	3	3	3	1	1	19	184·54

This outcome, incidentally, emphasizes that the aggregate points and placements (ordinals) are not determining factors, but are usually a good guide except when the issue is so close. Once again, Cousins could hardly have been denied the gold by a closer margin.

The 1979 European Championships, beginning in late January, occasioned my second visit to Zagreb, having previously competed there in the corresponding event in 1974. That had been the first competition in which I had suffered injury, so this time I was returning, hopefully not to repeat the injury but to enjoy the contest more and with the aim of impressing the judges well enough to earn another medal.

We arrived at the Inter-Continental Hotel, settled in and started training. Right from the beginning, it appeared the Yugoslavians had become British citizens. To me they did not seem like Yugoslavs at all, having apparently adopted me as their own. It was all very flattering and I was thrilled; not only

With Debbie Cottrill in Zagreb during the 1979 European Championships

did I have people back home in Britain rooting for me, but also these locals right here.

So I was very disappointed when, on the first day of the contest, I blew the figures back to Denver. I had not skated that badly the whole week. Others felt that I had been doing good enough figures during the practice to win, but when the vital time came, the tracings just did not go where they should have gone.

I was not at all happy with what I had done. Sixth place in the figures was one lower than I had achieved the year before, so an uphill task had to be faced in the short and long programmes. Carlo was unable to be at the Championships, because the United States Nationals were being held the same week. I think that even had he come to Zagreb, I might have been spending the remainder of the meeting without a coach, because probably he would have returned to Denver on the first available plane.

But Christa, being the wonderful lady she is, took it in her stride, was very calm and simply said: 'That's it, we'll just have to go on from here.' So, the following day with the short programme, I realized that I had nothing to lose and everything to gain. Although I was lying in sixth place, the third-, fourth-, fifth- and sixth-placed skaters were virtually tied on points and placements, so there was a possibility I could jump a position or two.

I skated what I think was my best short programme to date and came off with a perfect score from one judge and first place from all nine, to finish the second day in third overall spot. Obviously, at this point, everyone was beginning to wonder whether it was close enough. Was there a chance that I could pull up to second, or maybe even first? I was just happy that I was already in a medal position and hoped that I could hold on to it the following day.

The next morning's practice was little less than a disaster. Although I started out moderately well, it gradually deteriorated. I was being helped along on the sidelines by John Curry, who was in Zagreb to do commentary for American television. I began to feel a little pressure and ended the training session sprawled flat on my face in the middle of the rink.

At least I was happy to get some falls, stumbles and trips out of the way. They say a good performance can follow a bad rehearsal, and so it proved. I was tense, I was nervous, but the audience of some 5000 or 6000 were very much for Robin Cousins, so I felt almost under obligation to skate well for them, if only to make up for my doing so badly at the beginning of the competition.

I received two more perfect marks and was very, very happy with the performance. I lost my concentration just before the end of the programme. It had been very hard for me. I thought every movement through and, with about twenty seconds to go, I said to myself, 'that's it, everything's over, you've got a free and easy ride to the end,' but in reality, on my final jump I almost hit the deck. So far as nearly everybody else was concerned, it looked fine, but other skaters would have noticed that everything was not quite right and I think it was because I just did not concentrate right up until the final note of the music.

But I was otherwise content with the performance and, although once more I was made the winner of this section by all the judges, it still left me in final third place. Still, it was a better third than I had had the year before, in fact finishing with the highest aggregate points, a bronze medal overall and a gold for the free skating. But I was also in a very good position to upset everybody in the World Championships to follow in Vienna.

David Santee, the American I found so difficult to outpoint in the figures

Cousins caused his fans more nail-biting with a see-sawing start to his quest for the men's title when the sixty-ninth World Figure Skating Championships opened in March, 1979 in the spacious Stadthalle in Vienna, a city steeped in skating history.

After the three compulsory figures, he ranked fifth among the closely packed leaders, with no one in real command. With two-thirds of the competition still to come, Jan Hoffmann, winner in 1974, had emerged with a miniscule lead over Kovalev, the 1977 victor.

Two Americans, David Santee and the title defender, Charles Tickner, were third and fourth, but the top five were separated by only a fraction over three points — a now familiar pattern which promised much tension ahead.

In his first figure, the forward counter, the turns of Cousins were good, but one circle was slightly mis-shapen and he was marked fourth best behind Kovalev, Hoffmann and Tickner.

The second figure was the main psychological hurdle for Cousins. The paragraph bracket was the one he had spoiled with that crucial error which had denied him the European title five weeks earlier in Zagreb.

This time, he mastered the situation well. His manner of execution, flow, running edge and style were noticeably better. Hoffmann won this figure and took the lead, followed by Kovalev and Tickner, with Cousins still a fairly buoyant fourth.

Always his own sternest critic, Cousins was not only satisfied, but pleased. In a much better frame of mind, he looked forward to the third figure, the paragraph loop, but it was not so impressive, with the loops disproportionately small. With Hoffmann again top scorer in the loop, Santee entered the scene as next best, to overhaul both Tickner and Cousins.

Erratic marking from some judges — one even placed the Frenchman, Jean-Christophe Simond, first and Hoffmann only sixth — opened the issue even wider, but it was clear that any of the top five remained in with a real chance.

The middle stage of the contest next day was packed with incident. No fewer than four of the five overnight leaders failed in the multiple jump combination of the short free skating. Hoffmann did a single toe salchow instead of the requisite double. Santee fell from a double toe loop. Both Tickner and Cousins crashed when trying triple toe loops. Only Kovalev survived without a spill, and shakily at that. This unbelievable sequence of errors by such a talented assembly left Kovalev the new leader, with Hoffmann second, Tickner third and Cousins fourth, all less than five points apart.

Other noteworthy free skaters who tumbled included the Japanese, Fumio Igarashi, and Simond. More than one frustrated coach queried whether the surface was at fault, but Cousins said: 'No, the ice was good. Five of us were in such close contention. We were all so aware how important the combination was. You can put it down to tension.'

The big question on the night of the long free was whether Kovalev could be caught and, if so, by whom. It was not to be, but Robin Cousins at least became the first British figure skater for forty years to win a silver medal in the men's World Championship.

Before a crowd held in suspense in Vienna, the Bristolian magnificently over-hauled Hoffmann, the European Champion, and Tickner, the title defender, who finished third and fourth respectively, but he narrowly failed to catch the Russian.

The previous British silver medallist was Freddie Tomlins, who was runner-up to Graham Sharp in 1939. The only two British victories since the event began in 1896 were by Sharp and, in 1976, John Curry.

Cousins also had, once again, the satisfaction of winning a supplementary gold medal for the best free skating performance. He included three triple jumps and every aspect of his intelligently devised programme was brilliant – and his spins were superb.

Kovalev's performance was less distinguished. It may be unfair to suggest that Kovalev did not deserve to win, but correct to point out that he was only fourth best in the final free skating – behind Cousins, Tickner and Hoffmann, in that order.

The Russian owed his victory entirely to the fact that he maintained equilibrium during that disastrous short free skating session, when each of his three main rivals made, for them, unusual jumping errors because of the tension. Kovalev also had the luck to skate last and know that a careful performance without undue risk might be adequate, a philosophy he could not have dared adopt had he skated earlier in the order. The three immediately behind him would be unlikely ever to present him with a similar 'gift'.

I had been to Vienna twice before to skate, but only for exhibitions during the Vienna Cup competitions in September. What I had seen previously of this city I had liked very much, so I was looking forward to going back. The World Championship was going to be very hard. Charlie Tickner, the defending World Champion from the United States, was going to be there. Jan Hoffmann, Vladimir Kovalev and myself were to renew battle after finishing in that order in Zagreb. Fumio Igarashi, who had beaten Tickner a few months earlier in the Skate Canada internationals in Vancouver, would be full of confidence. Yes, it had the makings of a very tough competition.

Practice went very well and, come the first day of the Championships, I was quite satisfied with the way things were going. I was well pleased with the first two figures, as were Carlo and Christa Fassi, and I felt that I could have been a little better rewarded for them than I was. Everyone had become so accustomed to my not doing such good figures that, when I did put better ones down, it was hard for them to believe it.

The ice was a bit of a problem in Vienna, especially for the figures. It was very hard and a lot of snowy flakes were being brought up by the blades. This was obvious in the third figure, the loop, especially with regard to myself and Charles Tickner. We were getting stuck in our own tracings and it almost caused me to put my foot down – and did, in fact, cause Tickner to put his foot down. So we had twelfth and sixteenth places respectively in this particular figure, which was not very pleasing, but because both of us had been well up in the first two figures it made little difference to the final figures order, and I found myself ending a fairly respectable fifth in the figures.

I was going into the short programme with the feeling that I had a distinct chance of a medal. As to what colour it might be – well, we had to wait and see how everything went between now and the end of the event. But I was sitting in a good spot. Kovalev, Hoffmann and Tickner were all above me, but were all capable of making mistakes, as I was too. Igarashi was behind us and the French boy, Jean-Christophe Simond, was immediately in front of me. Simond had done a good job in Zagreb, where he had won the silver medal for free skating. So all seemed set for a very keen affair.

I think nerves took hold of everybody and all felt the pressure. I do not believe I have ever seen so many people fall or make so many mistakes in one competition at this level, as happened in the short programme of the men's event in Vienna. Kovalev skated in his usual restrained way and made no mistakes. Hoffmann made a mistake in the combination. Both Tickner and myself fell when landing our combinations. Scott Cramer came from behind and took second place in the short free. Simond was another to fall, as did Igarashi, and many of the lower placed performers also sat on the ice at one point or another.

It was a very difficult afternoon with a lot of stupid mistakes, and I think we realized afterwards how ridiculous and how silly we were. But I think it was something that çould have happened to anybody and, in this instance, happened to nearly everyone. So, the following night with the long programme, we had almost the opposite situation, where everybody skated very well, and I think we had been so disappointed with our performances the day before that we felt obliged to do something about redeeming ourselves.

I skated near the end, so did not get to see the other competitors skate. I made one big error and that was sitting in the dressing-room, where the audience's reactions were magnified. I concluded that everyone was skating absolutely flawlessly and that all the spectators had gone wild with delight. But it was not quite like that. I was told afterwards that the people I had concluded to have skated superbly had indeed performed well, but not so well as I had assumed. Regular applause for all had conveyed a false impression, which put extra pressure on me and caused me to become a little more nervous than I otherwise might have been.

Nevertheless, I skated well. It was OK. I was glad I didn't fall or make any disastrous mistakes. I know I can skate much better than I did in Vienna. Although I was very pleased with the silver medal, I think I could have won the championship if I had not fallen the day before. But if I had skated without

Vladimir Kovalev, World Champion in 1977 and 1979

error in the short programme, I could have easily fallen in the long. *Que será, será*.

In Vienna, I was accompanied by my parents, my brother Martin and a contingent of Bristol supporters and other people who had come from all parts of Britain, Scotland included, travelling in organized groups. On the Saturday after the championship, a reception was given for me by the proprietor of the Hotel Am Brillentengrund, where my parents and some of the British groups stayed. This is typical of Austrian hospitality and they presented me with a beautiful crystal bowl and a brochure signed by everyone in the hotel. I was glad to learn that, all in all, Vienna was a very successful trip for my supporters, who apparently had a super week.

13
A Royal Gala

The 1979 world tour of exhibition skating by the Vienna medallists and other leading performers was a pretty tough assignment because of the crowded schedule. It was a very busy, whirlwind tour, with most of the time spent travelling, sleeping or skating. It was also a very quick tour. We were sometimes in and out of cities the same day. We began by driving through Vienna to Bratislava, then back to Graz in Austria, thence to Prague, Ljubljana, Dresden, Karl-Marx-Stadt, London, Amsterdam, The Hague, Oslo, Helsinki, Copenhagen, Munich, Kiev, Leningrad and Moscow.

Unlike the previous year, when we were very much a show, this time we reverted to a loosely-strung series of individual performances. Only three times (in London, Munich and Helsinki) did we skate in a show atmosphere that included spotlights.

It was evident that the Russians were not allowed to be as friendly as they would have liked. When we sat eating, it was very noticeable that the East Germans and Russians would each sit at their own separate tables while the rest mingled more freely. Eventually, about mid-way through the tour, one of the Soviet ice dance couples started to sit and eat with us and we were getting on very well with them and having a super time – until they were told that they should be sitting with their compatriots and not mixing with us.

This was unfortunate, because they were trying to be friendly, and it was a pity that this enforced division limited our social activities. But we all enjoyed going to so many different cities, some that I had never seen before, and it was interesting too to observe how the various audiences reacted.

I was not very impressed with Russia. It was near the end of the tour, when everyone was tired, and I think after our three-and-a-half days there everybody was ready to go home and have a break. There was one awful train ride through the night from Leningrad to Moscow, during which hardly anyone had any sleep at all.

Even so, these world tours obviously provide memorable experiences and are, on the whole, great fun, though a considerable strain. Even after two-and-a-half weeks of it, you are still expected to be on top form and to be skating well, because the people who only see you that one night when you are at their rink, can easily overlook the fact that you have probably been skating every night for the last three weeks in different cities.

But the world tour is something special anyway. Each year, it comprises basically just the world medallists, touring either Europe or America or Asia, depending where the championships are held. Everyone tries to be on top form despite the strain, each aware that reputations must somehow be maintained. As the World Free Skating Champion, I was expected to be the best each night, so I really had no chance at all to ease up on what I did or how I did it. Towards the end of such a tour, it is not easy to look as fresh as you did at the beginning.

At the same time, it is a help to give exhibitions. You feel unrestricted because there are no judges and no limits to what you can skate. So, although I love competing and the element of competition is, obviously, most important, exhibitions are normally a pleasure to do.

After leaving East Germany, we arrived in London and, all of a sudden, we realized it was going to be *the* occasion of the tour. Not only was it a chance for us to skate before HM The Queen, who is the patron of the National Skating Association of Great Britain, but it was doubly auspicious, this being the Association's centenary year – and the world tour part of the celebration.

I was very honoured finally to meet past British world champions who came from far and wide especially for the event. Many had been only names to me until then. Cecilia Colledge I had met previously, but to see people like Megan Taylor and Graham Sharp for the first time was quite memorable. It was good also to renew acquaintance with Bernard Ford and Diane Towler, and to skate alongside an old team-mate, John Curry.

As we warmed up on the ice during the afternoon preceding the exhibitions, it became clear that the night was destined to be a very big one. Extra effort was made to ensure that the music and lighting would be correct and that all else would be right when the Queen arrived. Everybody was instructed to get into their right positions when the time came for presentations. We were informed that every seat had been sold for the Wembley Arena, which was hardly surprising in the circumstances.

While attendants fussed about and re-checked every little detail and flowers were placed meticulously in planned positions, it became evident that we were all getting a little nervous with the knowledge that we were to perform before such a large crowd – in London, a very knowledgeable one, and – above all, before the Queen and Prince Philip.

It is difficult to recall what is said to you by someone as important as the Queen because you cannot easily take it all in. But I do remember that she said it was

Carlo Fassi in reflective mood with Christa

nice for them finally to be able to come and see skating 'live'. The British have had little opportunity to watch such an array of skating talent except on television and, as Her Majesty said, it was enjoyable at last to come to somewhere like Wembley to see the skaters in the flesh.

We, as skaters, felt very honoured to have the Queen pay this personal tribute to our sport – and we were relieved that nobody made any notable errors that night. Prince Philip echoed the Queen's observation, adding how much better one can appreciate the speed, the height of the jumps and the gracefulness when the action is 'live'. Yes, Wembley really was the highlight of the tour.

*   *   *

Carlo Fassi is a businessman. His job is to make champions. I was very pleased when I was invited to join him and his wife, Christa, in Denver to train. It was an opportunity that I thought was too good to be missed. I had seen them working and had seen what they had done with John Curry, Dorothy Hamill and other skaters.

He is a tremendous coach. He has this knack of being able to produce exactly what he wants when he wants it. In training, even when you are skating well, you always feel that you can do better, that you can produce that little bit extra – and he can draw it right out of you.

One good thing about having two people to work with is that, after you have been working for a while with someone like Carlo, who sees the same mistakes over and over again, sometimes they get missed. You can be told the same thing repeatedly, but you cannot always translate it into the skating, so he is able to bring in someone like Christa, who can say the same thing in a different way that you are better able to understand. You interpret it differently, and these little things help.

Christa is very German and sometimes tends to be a lot harder than Carlo, which is not a bad thing. She is a 'finisher-offer'. She likes perfection in the movements and in the way that the lay-out of the programme is put together.

Carlo has excellent technique, especially in the compulsory figures, and since being with him I learned very much about how figures are supposed to be done. It is very easy to skate compulsory figures without properly understanding them, and this I believe was one of my shortcomings – I really did not understand what I was doing. But since I joined Carlo, I acquired a much better understanding of the figures – as well as jumping techniques and free skating generally.

At first, it was a little difficult to follow Carlo, because of his Italian accent, and I found that many things he said could be interpreted two or three different ways. But eventually I found I was able to translate to the ice what he was saying as he said it, without having to think too much. He is a wonderful person to have around at a competition, a tremendous morale booster and very good at giving you confidence. Even if you are not skating well, he lets you know when he is upset at the way you are skating, but at the same time can still make you want to do better and not feel dispirited.

I didn't expect him to react the way he does at competitions. I had the preconceived idea that someone who had had so many good skaters under his wing in the past, so many world and Olympic champions, would be a little blasé over a result such as a bronze medal at a European championship, let

Britain's Bernard Ford and Diane Towler, four times World Ice Dance Champions, with free leg actions in typically graceful unison

124

alone someone who just skates well in a minor competition. But his reaction is the same no matter who the skater is or what the event.

If you skate well, Carlo is jumping up and down beside the barrier as if you were the first person he has had who has ever done well, and it can be a joy to come off the ice and look at his face – because you can tell instantly whether he is pleased or not. He loves to show off his pupils, and when we go to competitions like a little troupe – his own private circus – he likes everyone to know that we are his charges and that he is showing us off to our best advantage.

Carlo and Christa are very different in temperament. Although they complement each other when they are working together, Christa is always there to calm down Carlo if he is getting too nervous before a competition – and Carlo is always there to say 'take it easy' to us if we are doing too much. They are both very dramatic over the training and over presentation at competitions. This is all part of their job as they see it, to make sure you do what is necessary at a competition regardless of whether you are on or off the ice, and I feel very relaxed when I am with them at an event. I feel that all I have to do is to get on to the ice and perform as they would want me to perform, and anything else that needs to be done is done by Carlo and Christa.

Free skating with Carlo is a matter of finishing everything off. I went to him knowing basically how I was doing my jumps with the triples and doubles, but Carlo made sure that every time I do a jump, it is technically correct. When we work out the programmes, he will decide whether the jumps are in the right place, as far as the judges are concerned – according to where they will be sitting.

I have learned a lot about finishing things off and putting things together properly since I have been with Carlo and Christa and I think that in the years that I have been with them, they have each played a very big part in my growing up on the ice, so to speak.

With the overall standard of skating as high as it is today, I think it is going to be necessary in the future for the judges to use the tenths of the point more realistically. It seems that the best compulsory figure has been rating about 4·4, while the average free skating mark is becoming a 5·7 or a 5·8 even for the skater who is finishing eighth or ninth. So, with the standard that we now have, it is important that the judges make more use of their tenths and bring the marks for free skating down to the same sort of ratio as the figures. That way, they will not restrict themselves – as has happened – to a situation where, with five free skaters to go, there is a margin of only two tenths of a point in which to separate them.

Some judges do tend to get themselves in a bit of a mess when they use their high marks too early, and this can affect the results of a competition. I am not saying it has or it will, but I believe, especially now that so many free skaters are so talented, the judges are going to have to be more careful how they use

In Helsinki during the world medallists' tour of 1979

high marks. The problem does not arise in the figures, so why should it in
free skating?

During my training in England, my social life was almost non-existent,
mainly because of the unsociable hours that I was keeping, having to skate when
the public were not. As a skater, I was often on my own and it was not until I
went to America and began training with skaters of my own age and people who
liked the same things, that I had any real off-the-ice life. Now I look forward to
going back to see my friends there. At the weekends or at any other time when
we are not skating, we would go swimming or drive up into the mountains for
an afternoon, or four or five of us would take some of the girls to the disco.

I love discos, and most of the skaters there are good dancers with good
appreciation of the music. The discos in America are very good, and I am lucky
that most of the girls also like the music. The people I relaxed with are also
skaters. We all had our own work to do on the ice, so it was good to be able
to go out as friends and have friendly relationships without being tied down,
so to speak. When you are in to something as heavily as I have been into skating,

127

you cannot really think of doing anything but train or skate. Fortunately, my skating friends in Denver were all doing the same thing for the same reason, so when we have been out socially together, we were just a bunch of skaters being 'regular kids'.

I found more time for reading than might be expected. A book I particularly enjoyed was one that I thought I would never even start, let alone finish – *Shogun* by James Cavill. It was recommended to me first of all by the Wylies and then by Christa Fassi, and it proved to be one of the most fascinating books that I have ever read, about sixteenth-century Japan, over a thousand pages of spellbinding reading. I also enjoyed *Taipan*, about China by the same author. When I was younger, I used to read spooky horror stories, and when I go to the movies now I like horror films or a good comedy, but hate westerns.

I appreciate old musicals; huge productions like those starring Gene Kelly and Fred Astaire. I remember vividly one particular dance sequence in a Gene Kelly–Judy Garland film called *The Pirate*. The scene was on board ship and the whole set was aflame when Gene came flying through the air in swash-buckling style to do a tremendous dance number. Another masterpiece of choreography, for me, was also by Gene Kelly in *An American in Paris*. I think it must be very difficult to recreate on film a dancing sequence which, on the stage of a live theatre, owes so much to the atmosphere and the audience. Even though *An American in Paris* is a vintage movie, the dance sequences in it are still very much in touch with what goes on today.

Live shows are for me a rich experience. I like anything to do with the theatre. *Chorus Line* was one of the finest entertainments that I have seen on Broadway, New York. Also, on Broadway I saw the Bob Fosse *Creation of Danc'n*, with new choreographic ideas which I found inspiring.

A stage show I liked in London was *Annie*, starring Sheila Hancock, who was very funny in a delightful escapade. Ballet naturally appeals to me and I have fond memories of Barushnikov, the Russian ballet dancer, living in the States. He is so perfect on film that I wonder how many 'takes' it requires to achieve such exactness. Maybe I would get a better idea about that if I were to see him on the stage.

I once saw Margot Fonteyn dance in Bristol and, although past her peak, she was still in total command on that stage from the moment she stepped on until the moment she stepped off – and it is the same thing that you try to do on the ice. The moment you step on the ice, the minute the music starts, you try to take command of everything that is there – and you have an obligation to maintain command and to keep hold of the audience until you stop skating, until you leave the ice. Then, it does not matter what they do. They can turn around, they can talk, but I think it is one of the nicest things to know that, in the middle of your programme, every single person in that stadium is watching you. No one is talking, no one has gone to get a hot dog or ice cream – they are watching you perform – and it is the same with the theatre. You take command of every little detail around you and try to keep hold of that until the last note has gone.

It is no different skating now from what it was before I had the operations. The removal of cartilage has left me, my physiotherapist said, with second class knees. But, so far as I am concerned, they are no different from the ones I had before. There is nothing to prevent either cartilage from starting to grow again at any time, and perhaps either cartilage on the *outside* of my knees could also give me problems – so I am not totally immune to any more trouble simply because I have had these two operations. But they have 'done their job.' In years to come, hopefully, I may be able to go without any more injuries of this kind.

As a Bristolian, it was very gratifying to be honoured with a civic reception by the Mayor and Mayoress and fellow councillors of the city of Bristol at the Mansion House on April 24th, 1979. It was, they said, a tribute to my achievements during the past year, which had included the world silver medal. What pleased me particularly was that my parents were invited also to this public lunch, as well as my former coach, Pam Davies. They had all contributed so much towards my achievements and it was good to have them share in this kind of home-town gesture.

Because I spent most of my time in recent years outside my own country, I was largely unaware of the publicity given to me in my absence. But when I arrived home on brief visits, I was suddenly enmeshed by the media, with interviews for newspapers, radio and television, and with invitations to appear here, there and everywhere – so much so that time at home shrunk to much shorter periods than I or my parents might have wished.

Not that I minded. I have felt very honoured that people should bother to ask me and I think it is only fair that when you are in the public eye – obviously, for me, on a very small scale compared with lots of people – you should feel ready and willing to fulfil these obligations to the public by giving interviews and attending the various functions so far as time will reasonably permit. But I never really expected it to reach such limits – and it has seemed very odd for me suddenly to find myself having to say 'sorry, I don't have time' to some people with whom I would willingly have spent hours a couple of years earlier, when publicity for myself and the sport was at a premium.

One of my major boosts, for what seemed likely to be the final year of my competitive career, was the presentation to me by the Sports Aid Foundation of the Sir Jack Cohen Memorial Award. Cohen was the founder of Tesco Stores, which runs a lottery in Britain for the Sports Aid Foundation, the proceeds to be given yearly to a sportsman or sportswoman considered worthy of this grant. Fortunately for me, the amount covered the difference between

129

what my sponsorship and my parents were paying for me to train. So the award meant that, for the season of the 1980 Olympics, all my financial worries were taken from my parents and I was able to return to Denver, happy in the knowledge that sufficient money was available to pay for all my training needs without any more burden to the family.

Of course, I do not see any cash of this kind. It has to be paid through my National Skating Association, to comply with strict regulations governing amateur status. In some of the other sports, it is possible for amateurs to earn money in various ways but for skaters, even when we are doing shows and exhibitions, it is impossible in Britain to make any money from skating and remain an amateur.

It has been a long time since we were able to compete with the Russians and East Germans so far as training and aid is concerned, but now, with the kind of assistance beginning to come from the Sports Aid Foundation, British competitors in the future may get more of a chance to compete on level terms in this respect.

14
The Big Season Build-up

The summer of 1979 in the United States was very agreeable, alternating serious training with recreation. I prepared for the season ahead for anything up to seven hours a day on the ice, plus two or three hours off it – the latter including regular dance training, stretch exercises, running, jogging and anything else I thought might help to get myself in peak condition.

I started around 8 a.m., skating every hour with a twenty-minute break between then and 1.30 p.m. In the afternoons, I was either out running or over at the dance studio – and that usually took another two or three hours. Then I would be back at the rink, probably from 6 p.m. until 8 p.m., getting home about half-past eight.

If you become slack in your training, especially with running through the programmes or keeping yourself in condition, then it is difficult to get sufficient breath on the day of a competition. But training as we did in Denver, at an altitude of a mile high, we had to get ourselves in shape very early. Otherwise, we would have been in trouble from high-altitude sickness.

So we did a lot of running and physical training during the first couple of days after arrival, before we even started to skate. Without such precautions, a badly affected throat can develop and this can lead to being off the ice for a week or so until it clears up. Most of the skaters therefore make sure they get in good condition. I think for any sport it is very important that you are physically fit before you even start to think about doing what you have to do for competitions.

I am often asked if spinning makes me giddy. The only time I feel giddy is when I close my eyes. It is surprising that, in spite of the speed, unlike ballet dancers you are not spotting; you are just letting your body take its own force. You still manage to pick up a light or a flash of colour somewhere in the arena that keeps you from feeling dizzy, because otherwise you lose your sense of where you are.

But it is important that you centre yourself on the right position of the blade, to be able to make the small circles without travelling halfway up the rink at the same time. That is something the judges are looking for – whether you stay in the same place or travel too far.

My biggest thrill of the whole summer was going to the Broadmoor Arena at Colorado Springs and skating in their amateur show. At the time, my brother Nick was over on vacation. He had spent a couple of days with me in Denver, and the two of us went to Broadmoor together.

The show ran for a whole week, which included my birthday, so I had a special party at the Broadmoor. It was good that finally a member of the family was able to see where I was living and training in America and I looked forward to the prospect of my parents being able to get out to Denver after the Olympics.

Nick was able to see the people I lived with and the Denver rink. He was surprised at the rink because he expected it to be more glamorous, but he saw that the ice and training facilities were good, and how everyone worked together and helped each other.

The Colorado Ice Arena is a good training centre but purely functional, as distinct from many of the ice rinks in England, where they have flashing lights, coke and pin-table machines. These are lacking at the CIA and even at Broadmoor – which is a much more glamorous arena, with more seating, yet still just an ice rink and nothing else, which I think is what they should be.

The Broadmoor Hotel, its multi-sports complex, everything in the vicinity is gorgeous, but it is very much a retreat for retired, wealthy people who like to come and spend their weekends (or weeks) at golf and sit by the heated outdoor swimming pool and maybe talk about the stock exchange. It is very plush, not the type of place that many youngsters stay at, except when invited to participate in sports events. In contrast to the frenzied movement of the ice show, a stone's throw away beside the adjoining lake, the hotel is elegant and everything seems to be going at a snail's pace. I was at the Broadmoor for my first World Championships four years previously. I like Broadmoor. I like Colorado Springs.

Earlier in Denver, I had been pleased to be joined by Karena Richardson in May. I had asked Carlo if he would be able to teach her. Basically, she wanted to try and get her confidence back and be able to reach a good enough level to regain her British title which, following a three-year reign, she had lost the previous December to Debbie Cottrill.

Carlo said yes. He had watched her and thought that she still had a lot of potential, so it was on May 8th that I went to Denver airport to welcome her. It was very good for both of us to have another Brit in the place. It certainly boosted Karena's morale to be among our friendly international gathering.

It was much nicer for me. I felt less on my own with a compatriot and we were able to enjoy each other's company both on and off the ice. Her progress too backed up my theory that the change of atmosphere and working under these conditions can really improve and enhance one's performance.

The Carlo Fassi entourage in Denver. Standing, from left to right, Carlo, Anne-Sophie de Kristoffy (France), Jean-Christophe Simond (France), Barbara Toffalo (Italy), Garnet Ostermeier (West Germany), Claudia Binder (Austria), Helmut Binder (Austria), Karena Richardson, me, Kristina Wegelius (Finland), and Christa. Kneeling, Hae-Sook Shin (South Korea), Emi Watanabe (Japan), and Reiko Kobayashi (Japan)

The second Rotary Watches Ice International, now an annual fixture, began on the English Thames-side rink at Richmond on 9th October, 1979. A keen competitive element among the women – between the East German, Dagmar Lurz, and the Japanese, Emi Watanabe, and, on the home front, between Karena Richardson and Debbie Cottrill – gave the crowd such entertaining fare that the appearance of Robin Cousins seemed like a luxury dessert.

The British Olympic gold medal hope did not disappoint, leading after the figures a field that included the Russian, Igor Bobrin, who had outpointed Cousins in the figures of the previous season's European Championships. To lead Bobrin at this stage was as much as any Cousins supporter could have wished for in normal circumstances. But this day's were hardly normal.

The wonder is that he skated at all. It says much for the courage of Cousins that few onlookers had any idea that the British Champion had passed a sleepless night following great discomfort from food poisoning. Only the most vigilant eye could discern slight discrepancies in his tracings. If Cousins could perform figures like he did this day while much under the weather, one wondered how much better he might fare when fully fit.

Later the same day, he handsomely consolidated the advantage with a short free skating performance difficult to fault.

Bobrin and the Canadian, Brian Pockar, just could not match the lanky Englishman in full flow. The highlight of his seven obligatory elements was, as usual, the jump combination, this time linking double loop and daringly high triple toe loop jumps which, thanks to masterly technique, were made to look so deceptively simple.

'I don't know how I did it,' said Cousins afterwards. 'I started being sick at about 11.30 last night and I've hardly stopped since. I had no option but to skate, although I felt terrible throughout the day – and I still do.' Throughout his career Cousins had proved remarkably resilient, constantly rising like a Phoenix from the flames of adversity to confound the critics.

Bristol skaters excelled the next day. While Cousins demolished all male opposition with consummate ease, his fellow home-towners, Robert Daw and Susan Garland, gained a bronze medal in the pairs event.

Free from championship tension, Cousins treated his fans to an electrifying preview of his Olympic long free programme, performed with evident relish and rapturous abandon. As if without a care in the world, he never put a foot wrong while executing some of the most difficult jumps in the book, his outwardly carefree manner of presentation belying a meticulously prepared order of technical contents.

He included four different triples – toe loop, loop, salchow and toe salchow – without betraying any physical weakness from his earlier misfortune. So much is made of his outstanding jumping that one tends sometimes to forget that he is also the world's best and most versatile spinner.

Bobrin, the Soviet runner-up, also reached a high level in more senses than one. Without Cousins, he could have been highly acclaimed, but even his skilful efforts suffered by comparison with the sport's man of the moment. Pockar clinched a close-fought third place from the Japanese, Mitsuru Matsumura, while Chris Howarth, Britain's likely Olympic number two, ended an encouraging sixth.

This first public try-out by Cousins of his new programme destined for Lake Placid was an unqualified success. 'I don't intend to change anything,' he said, and Christa Fassi nodded happily in agreement: 'We are already satisfied with the arrangement and will now concentrate on improving the quality.'

What impressed particularly was his final, stamina-demanding forty-five seconds – packed with non-stop jumps and spins performed at bewildering pace. This tremendous climax was somehow managed despite his earlier ailment. Surely, one surmised, nobody can now stop a fully fit Cousins in full song.

At the Skaters' Ball with Karena Richardson

The 1979 Rotary event was important to me because (a) I was finally going to get a chance to compete internationally in my home country, which I had not been able to do the year before because I was injured, and (b) it was the first competition of the big Olympic season.

So, naturally, I wanted to do well. I had been working very hard during the summer. I was looking forward to coming home. I was in very good physical and mental shape and was skating as well as I thought I was capable of doing at the time.

I was not worried, but eager to get reactions to the new programme, to find whether or not it needed changes and how things were going. Unfortunately, it was to be yet another competition with a setback, this time through sickness – a virus of some kind I picked up the night before the event began – yet it may have helped in a curious way.

Christa seemed to think that, because I was so sick, I was in a sense less worried – that is to say, I was more worried about myself than about my figures. So that morning I laid down what for me were three excellent figures, better than I had done in a competition before, though still not as good as I had done in practice. They were sufficient for me to win the figures for the first time in an international competition.

I was very pleased, yet strangely too sick to worry about the rest of the contest to come. I could not practise that afternoon for the short programme, so I had to go out in the evening more or less cold, as it were, to perform the seven elements. Although I did everything as well as I could be expected to do at the time, I was still well below par yet managed to win fairly comfortably.

After eventually being able to get something to eat, keep it down and have a good night's rest, the following day I was feeling very much better for my long programme. As it happened, everything came off fine. I skated all as well as I could have done and was very pleased with the results. Everybody appeared to like the new programme. The judges seemed to be very much in favour of what I was doing and it went as well as I could have hoped.

Reflecting back to that hapless night before I was due to start, clearly I had eaten something that did not agree with my stomach. It had kept me up all night and I did not go to sleep at all. In fact, I rested sitting up in the bathroom, leaning against a pillow, because it was too far for me to run if I needed to get from my bed to the bathroom.

I spent the night awake and was really not in any condition to walk, let alone skate. The following day, all I had was glucose water to drink for something like fourteen hours, which at the time seemed unlikely to give me enough energy to compete, but somehow I managed.

I think the fact that I had been through so many mishaps in competitions, and this was just one more, prompted Carlo later to say nothing I ever do surprises him – either I am getting ill during a contest or falling and hurting my back or knee or scratching my leg – and I cannot pretend that he is wrong.

I do not remember much about my figures or the short programme of the Rotary event because of my condition. All I recall about the short programme is arriving. I do not even remember getting dressed – someone had to help. It was just a question of putting myself on the ice and doing what I had to do, then returning to the hotel to get some sleep.

It all seems so hard to believe now. I just assume that I did everything in the short free that I was supposed to have done, although it must have looked well under my usual par. But the following day in the long programme, I seemed to recover very rapidly and was able to put on a performance that reasonably matched what I was able to do in training and, fortunately, proved to be much better than I had dared to hope.

I went back to Denver after the Rotary competition for just two weeks of training before going to Tokyo for the NHK International Free Skating Competition. I was a little sceptical about returning to the scene of probably my biggest setback. I really did not know how I would feel skating there again and I was very surprised on arrival to realize how many people had remembered me, perhaps not so much for my skating as for my dramatic crawling off the ice.

My first practice in the Yoyogi Stadium was very different from what I had expected. I was nervous about performing there again. It was quite strange at first but, once over the initial shock and being apparently in good form I soon felt able to concentrate on the task at hand.

Although there were no figures, I was perhaps under more pressure than in London – free skating against Fumio Igarashi, an up-and-coming World Championship contender skating on home ice. So I was naturally a little wary about how well I would do or how well *he* would do.

As it happened, I managed to skate maybe not quite so well as I had in the free at Rotary, but well enough to gain wins in both short and long programmes. Carlo and Christa were with us in Japan and they had two winners, Emi Watanabe coming first in the women's contest.

The fact that there were no figures in Tokyo did not really bother me; ironically Igarashi's figures were not as good as mine, but he had beaten Tickner the previous season and had put up two very good free skating performances at the World Championships in Vienna. He was not one to be discounted just because I had beaten him in Vienna and I think one of the reasons Carlo made me go to Tokyo was to put me up against a challenge as strong as Igarashi. It seemed to pay off.

There was some criticism about my going to The Hague soon afterwards to compete in another international free skating competition, this time for the Ennia Challenge Cup. I had been invited to The Hague the previous year and had been unable to go, so early in 1979 I was asked again. Carlo said yes, it would be fine for me, before we realized what else I was going to be doing that far ahead.

The Hague subsequently put out some publicity for the TV to say that I was competing, so I decided to go anyway even though it was only a week before the British Championships. I assumed it was just something to keep me occupied so that I would not start to 'panic'. Carlo thought that the more I got out in front of the judges, the more I would get used to it and the less pressure I would feel I was under.

In the meantime, my National Association had found a sponsorship for the British Ice Dance Championship in Nottingham, which coincided with the competitions in Holland, and the sponsors were going to give a donation to the Association on condition that I skated an exhibition.

So I was in Holland for the short programme on the Thursday and established a satisfying lead. Then, on the Friday morning, I found myself flying from Amsterdam to Birmingham, being picked up by my parents and driven to Nottingham, where, on the Friday night, I did the exhibition which followed the dance championship.

Getting up at 5.30 a.m. on Saturday to drive down to Birmingham and fly back to Holland, I arrived at the hotel in The Hague around one o'clock, just two-and-a-half hours before competing in the competition's long programme. Needless to say, my performance was nowhere near the standard that I had produced in the two previous competitions. But everyone seemed to understand the circumstances.

A lot of people apparently had thought I would not return from England to finish the competition, but I was determined to keep my promise to do so and, fortunately, managed to win. The trip to Nottingham was something that I could have done without and I think it was unfortunate that I found myself under obligation to do more than Carlo or I thought was necessary.

I went to Nottingham because my National Skating Association told me to. They said I had no choice, but knew I was going to compete at The Hague. The annoying factor is that they had complained earlier about the number of exhibitions that I had been giving in America because of the tiring effect of the travelling involved. But the minute the Association stood to get something out of it, they were the ones to say yes and told the people concerned before even asking me. It was a bit of a bind, but I got through it.

The next week I spent in Bristol, preparing for the British Championships. Although it was good to be home, it was a little awkward trying to train to championship standard when the first hour of ice available was at midnight. For four days I trained from midnight to three in the morning in Bristol.

High spirits during the 1979 ISU world tour in The Hague as I help pull the leg of Linda Fratianne with (from left to right) Tai Babilonia, Randy Gardner and Astrid Jansen in der Wal

At Richmond during the last week of November 1979, Cousins made his defence of the British title look a mere formality. He appeared this time to be almost as confident in the figures as he always did in the free skating, but how much this was due to his undoubtedly improved tracings and how much to the lack of pressure was a moot point.

It is no disrespect to his closest rivals to observe that they could not offer a serious challenge, for there were now few in the world who could hope to stay in touch with Robin at any stage of a contest.

Although in a class on his own at Richmond, it was easy to discern that his figures had advanced appreciably, a heartening portent for the Winter Olympics.

The technical highlight of his short free skating was a superb combination of double loop and daringly high triple toe loop jumps, as if to suggest that it could be worth travelling a long way to see his final free skating the following night, but things did not quite turn out that way.

Cousins duly won his fourth consecutive national title, but on the last day of the event his customary panache was missing. He fell heavily from a triple toe loop jump and looked as surprised as any onlooker.

Though clearly shaken, he recovered enough to make ample amends, leaving his challengers struggling gamely but in vain. Chris Howarth was an impressive runner-up, with Andrew Bestwick third.

Cousins said afterwards: 'I am not too disappointed by tonight's form. I well remember that John Curry also had a fall when he was winning the British title for

139

the fourth time – and that was in the same season that he went on to win gold medals in the Olympic, European and World Championships. So maybe this is a good omen.'

The reason for his lapse was probably because earlier he had been attempting too much. During the preceding four weeks, he had entered and won relatively unimportant international competitions in Tokyo and The Hague – even commuting from the middle of the latter to fit in an exhibition at Nottingham.

He might instead have rested to avoid the risk of overdoing things during the vital run-up to the Olympics. Perhaps the below-par Richmond performance proved a blessing in disguise, because he immediately cancelled plans to spend the following fortnight in Australia.

It would have entailed several exhibitions, pressure from the news media, travel weariness and, almost certainly, no time for the relaxation at first envisaged. He and those around him were wise enough to realize that, had he gone to Australia, all work and no play might easily have made Robin a dull boy.

I went to Richmond a few days before the British Championships were due to begin and Christa and Karena arrived from Denver. Karena was very nervous about trying to win back her title and I was just hoping that I could forget Holland and Nottingham and put up a performance worthy of probably my last national title defence and the one immediately preceding the European, Olympic and World meetings.

My first two figures were satisfactory. The loop I know I can do much better, but I was happy overall to win the figures and then to produce what I thought was the best short programme I had so far done. Unfortunately, there were very few people there to see it.

Going into the long programme, I had a big lead and had no inspiration to skate whatsoever. I had lost the inclination. I was very excited to have seen Karena skate well enough to win back her title and I suppose I was lacking adrenalin.

There was little for me to do to win and I tried very hard to push myself, to make myself go for a worthy performance. I remember standing by the rink barrier before going on the ice and thinking I did not really want to skate. It was not possible to pretend to myself that I was third or fourth and needed to push hard to come first. I had always found it much easier when coming from the back or when having some pressure behind.

Because I had no pressure, it was hard to get myself in the right mood. Anyway, when I tripped on the first triple toe loop and fell, that was it. I just wanted to get off and go home or get out and do something other than finish the programme. I had no inspiration and that is all I think I can say about the performance because, as far as I was concerned, it was rubbish.

I had not skated that badly for years, so was just happy to get it out of the way. As Christa said, you have to have one bad performance. Practically everything that could go wrong *did*. I was quite content with the figures and short free. It was only the long free that seemed to be a bit of a disaster. So half the event was good and half of it bad, a somewhat hollow victory.

I noticed at Richmond that, for the first time, the judges were sitting off the ice and this made things a lot easier. Richmond was not the biggest ice rink that we would be skating in and it does make a difference when the judges are behind the barrier. It is also easier for them because they are not going to get such cold feet.

From Richmond I went back to America and soon forgot about it. After a relaxing Christmas and New Year, I made slight alterations in the programme content – nothing drastic or different from the way I had been performing it.

I had been invited to Australia to give what had been assumed to be two or three exhibitions. It had been the idea of the Australian Cain family. The pair skaters, Peter and Elizabeth Cain, had spent some training time with me and I was really looking forward to seeing their country for the first time. As things turned out, my tiredness following the British Championships led to the plan being cancelled, but I hoped to take up the invitation and go to Australia later.

I did not prepare myself for the 1980 Olympic year in any special way, but just the same as I would for any other season. I tried not to think about it being anything different from a normal skating year.

The short programme music, *The Railway Children*, which I had used in 1977 and 1978 but not in 1979, was revived for 1980. The reason I did that was because Carlo told me to. By this time, I hated it. After skating to it for two years and dropping it for a year, I brought it back simply because it was catchy, something the audience liked, the judges liked and Carlo liked, but that I didn't any longer. There must be ballet dancers who cannot stand *Swan Lake* because they have danced it so many times that they have it coming 'out of their ears'.

By now I had done it so often that I would just put the music on, skate to it – and it always came out the same. I suppose it is very similar to the robot reaction, which is probably why I grew to detest it so much. I knew that every time the music went on, I did exactly the same thing in exactly the same place. But for the short programme that aspect did not really matter, because it is best that way. And I have rarely made any mistakes when doing it, touch wood.

I hope the judges appreciated how perfectly timed the whole thing became in the end. It was laid out very carefully and precisely. The music was cut right and everything was exactly what I consider it should be for a short free.

But the long programme is different. For 1980 I decided what I wanted to do and to what kind of music. I had had a somewhat classical programme the previous year and now I wanted something basically up-beat disco, mindful of its popularity. I may have veered towards pleasing an American audience, as opposed to European or British, mainly because of the Olympics and because I knew I would be performing a lot in the States and Canada.

Yet I still wanted to include some music that would give a classical air and maybe even produce something of everything – with a bit of jazz, disco, classical and romantic.

I did a lot of searching around before trying out three or four different pieces and then came across exactly what I wanted. The only piece I had known well in advance that I wanted to use was the ending – a modern rock jazz version of *Paint It Black*, which was originally a Rolling Stones hit and therefore going back quite a time, but this particular version appealed very much and was such a heavy orchestration that it sounded really good over the sound system of an ice rink.

An American disco group had a big hit out at the time and a friend of mine bought the album, which happened to have some music on the other side which sounded very different in the rink from what it did when I played it at the Wylies' home. I ended up using this for an opening – a sort of slinky, mood-setting piece leading into some disco music, very much the type you would expect to hear in a big stomping night club. I managed to cut it, using two recordings to get what I wanted.

So, with the beginning and the disco piece cut, I managed to contrast it by using something that Richard Rodney Bennett incorporated for the film, *Murder on the Orient Express*. People I told of my plans looked at me as if to say, what on earth are you doing putting all these pieces of music together; they don't sound as if they should match. But in fact they tended to complement each other very well and I complimented myself on the way that I had managed to put them together. It did not sound choppy or cut around and though each piece had a beginning and an end the whole sequence flowed from one to the other.

I was very lucky, because it took me less than a day to decide on the selection and it seemed to fall into place very easily, as did the programme. When I started to make up the skating with Christa it was just this goes here and that goes there, and we did not have to worry about what went in between – it all seemed to fall into place.

It was easily skateable music, very easy on the ear and very different from anything anyone else had. The order began with *Belle de Jour*, by a group called San Tropez, from an American album of the same name. Next came *Dragons at Midnight*, from a disco album by Mike Theodore. This was followed by *Murder on the Orient Express*, ending with the Johnny Harris version of *Paint It Black*.

15
Triple Crown Chance

An elated Robin Cousins held a very strong third position at the end of the compulsory figures in the 1980 European Championships at Gothenburg in January. This was three places higher than at the equivalent stage the year before.

Only Vladimir Kovalev, the Soviet World Champion, and Jan Hoffmann, the East German title defender, had kept above him -- and each by an inconsequential margin. So the prospects were extremely bright for a British victory if Cousins could repeat the previous season's clear superiority in the free skating.

In the tense and absorbing figures conflict with Kovalev and Hoffmann – none of the other twenty-one competitors were ever in the hunt – Cousins made a morale-boosting start, scoring second highest marks in the opening rocker figure.

Consistent throughout the compulsories, he was also second in the other two – paragraph bracket and paragraph loop – but because Kovalev won the first and third and Hoffmann the second, the overall difference between the three was effectively minimised.

Four of the five judges placed Cousins first, the other five opted for Kovalev, and Hoffmann – the lowest points scorer of the three – slotted incredibly between them.

'This is the highest I have yet finished after the figures in any international championship,' Cousins reminded us. He then dashed off to telephone his parents in Bristol. They expressed regret that they were unable to be with him because they had saved up to go to the following month's Lake Placid Olympics instead. 'Don't worry,' he told them. 'I'm going to do it all again there.'

That remark typified the confidence he had shown earlier, with no semblance of past nervous anxiety. There was now an air of quiet optimism in the Cousins camp. His coaches, Carlo and Christa Fassi, appeared well satisfied with their protégé's performance thus far. Both were aware that, barring the kind of mishap which can befall anyone in this hazardous sport, the Bristolian had the potential not only to make up the gap but to take the title.

But Cousins kept his supporters on tenterhooks when he missed a chance to leap into the lead on the second day. His intended linkage of double loop and triple cherry (toe loop) jumps to highlight the short free performance did not work out as planned.

At the last moment, he made the second jump a double. A triple jump in the combination is optional, but Kovalev succeeded with a triple salchow and Hoffmann managed a triple toe walley. None of the top three missed an obligatory element.

Double flip and double axel jumps were made to look deceptively simple by Cousins. His flying jump-camel spin, landing in a full sitting posture, was a delightful exercise of perfection. His straight line step sequence was full of fast, intricate footwork, timed superbly to music from *The Railway Children*. Despite such eloquence of movement, he was never quite in full flow in what, by his high standards, was something of an off day.

The official order remained Kovalev, Hoffmann and Cousins, but none would start the final free with any meaningful advantage.

In that final free, Robin gave the complete answer to his coach, who had called him 'chicken' the night before, by clinching the title with a performance of sparkling genius. Pulling out all the stops, he left Kovalev and Hoffmann both floundering helplessly in his wake.

Only two other Britons had won the title — Graham Sharp in 1939 and John Curry in 1976. Only twenty-four hours earlier, Fassi had publicly accused his star pupil of being 'chicken' for turning that intended triple jump into a double — a harsh description for the world's most courageous jumper, famed for some remarkably resilient returns after injury.

But Fassi afterwards admitted: 'I just said it to gee him up,' and he took the trouble to telephone Robin's parents to reassure them of his motive. The criticism had never seemed to worry Cousins. 'Don't worry, I've got everything under control,' he said before starting the crucial five-minute performance he knew would make or break his chance to emulate Curry's 1976 triple crown of European, Olympic and World triumphs.

Clearly, he had recovered composure after his much-publicized oversight of the day before. All his confidence had returned and he produced a scintillating performance, rich in multiple jumps and superb spinning artistry. Three triples were included — a loop and two cherries — in a display brought to a thrilling climax with a stamina-sapping final sixty seconds crammed with non-stop action.

He scored three maximum sixes for artistic impression — rightly implying perfection, for he made no error.

Kovalev included four triples — a loop, two salchows and a cherry — in an otherwise uninspiring performance for a World Champion. The Russian was clearly beaten and Hoffmann, who had yet to skate, must have known in his heart that he could not match a Cousins in such full song. The East German tried hard, featuring four triples — a lutz, two cherries and a loop — but the task was beyond him.

British Airways arranged my trip from Denver to Gothenburg for the 1980 European Championships and kindly offered to pay the extra costs for me to take the Concorde flight. So I flew from Denver to Washington and then took

Concorde from Washington to London, which was a tremendous experience.

The speed and the take-off are incredible. You are not aware of the flying time or the speed difference while you are in the air. The service is immaculate and it was not until I reached London that I realized my parents had been getting ready to leave Bristol to drive to London at the same time as I was leaving Washington – quite mind-boggling when you think of the contrast in distances.

I flew on from London to Milan, having arranged to be there for a week preceding the European Championships. Carlo was going to be away that week at the United States Championships and, as there was no ice available for training at the Gothenburg Scandinavium rink until three days before the meeting, the rink in Milan, the Palazzo del Ghiaccio, offered us ice for the week, when we put in some hard work with Christa.

On the day before we left Milan, Emi Watanabe went with me to La Scala to see Nureyev perform in *The Nutcracker*, which was a memorable experience. The Scala is one of the most beautiful theatres I have ever been in and it was marvellous to see someone like Nureyev dance.

We arrived in Gothenburg on the Friday, fit and in good form. I was satisfied with progress despite not having worked with Carlo for the week, but he was arriving in Gothenburg on the Sunday, two days before the championships started, so if there were any last-minute little details to be checked on, I knew he would be there to do it.

The couple of days before the championships did not prove too nerve-wracking. It seemed I was very much a centre of interest and onlookers appeared to watch my every training move to see how many times I was falling, if I was missing this, how I was skating that, whether I was doing all the jumps properly and whether I was doing anything fresh.

I think a lot of people were naturally anxious to see everyone's new programmes for the season, particularly with the Olympics to come. All this attention we managed to take in our stride and I felt quite confident the night before the competition began.

The draw for the figures was a group that I particularly liked and there was no reason for me not to do especially well in those figures, as I had been doing them well in practice. So, on the morning of the figures I didn't feel particularly worried and was almost in the same frame of mind as when I free-skate, which is quite unusual for me.

I laid down what I consider were probably the best figures I had ever traced in my life in competition, and it was unfortunate for me that they were not quite good enough to win the section. But I think our actual placings – the one, two and three – were immaterial. It was just so tightly packed, so far as the judges were concerned, because the three of us – Kovalev, Hoffmann and myself – had done consistently good figures.

145

It was therefore just a matter of who was going to put in the better free skating performance. I think I was still on an adrenalin high from the figures for the short programme. I was really not too conscious of what I was doing.

I had not had a very good time with the combination during the previous couple of days and for some reason I was just not even thinking about a triple toe loop in the combination when I did the short programme. As it happened, I came out with the double loop combined with a nice double toe loop. I do not know why; I did not even think about it at the time I did it.

It just happened and I hoped it would never happen again. But, when it eventually did sink in during the middle of the programme, I knew I had to have the rest as perfect as it was capable of being. Otherwise, I was really going to lose out.

I found myself in third place in the short programme, lower than I had been in three years. It was a strange feeling and unfortunate that I should let myself down like this. I knew then that I was going to have to push myself back up again with the long programme, which is something that I seem to enjoy doing to myself – always putting myself in these unnecessary predicaments.

I was not too worried about the position going into the long programme. I knew what I had to do to recover and Carlo had worked out what marks I needed to make up. Even though I had not made any mistakes the day before, I had not done what I had hoped.

With the short free, I think it is inevitable that judges will reduce marks for not doing a triple, but in fact not including a triple isn't an error: the required jump is a double jump and what you link it with is up to you (*i.e.* any double or triple). It so happens that what I did was probably the easiest combination anyway.

Why did I not do a triple? The question came up over and again. I just do not know. It was not my intention to do a double. I did not even realize at first that I had not done a triple.

The last thing I saw or heard of Carlo for a while when I came off the ice after the short programme was: 'What the hell do you think you did by –' and the door slammed behind him and I was left standing with Christa. What Carlo said the other side of the door became a minor sensation. I did not hear it myself. It was not addressed to me, but to someone who enquired what happened, Carlo apparently retorted: 'I don't know. He was just a big chicken' – which is something that Carlo and Christa would say many times every day of their lives to every kid that they teach.

So to us it was no big deal, but obviously one of the press reporters heard it and the next thing we knew it was all over the place. A lot of people said it was done on purpose, but so far as I was concerned it was not meant in the same manner that some interpretations suggested. I did not give it serious thought

Showing some of the confidence gained while living in the States

146

because I had heard the phrase addressed so often to all of us in Denver and it was nothing new.

The morning before the long free passed agreeably with satisfactory practice in the main rink. Previously, at the training rink some distance away, I had experienced a slight problem with the triple salchow. I never enjoyed skating at that training rink in Gothenburg – it always felt damp, cold and unfriendly. But I loved the Scandinavium arena in which the championships were held. Comfort and congeniality while you are skating makes all the difference.

The long free obviously went well and the marks were incredible from my point of view. I know I can be a lot better technically, but I think the presentation was one of my best and so I gained the European title.

I skated before Hoffmann and had to watch him go through. He really produced a very good performance, pulling out some nice jumps, but fortunately the judges went for me and I was very happy to win my first international championship.

The following night, after the ice dance championship, the significance of my win sunk home when it was announced: 'The next to give an exhibition will be the European Champion, Robin Cousins.' But on the Sunday at the traditional end-of-championship exhibitions, I was petrified at the thought of having to follow Rodnina and Zaitsev, which in my time was something that nobody had done before.

They always finished, and there was some controversy about the fact that the organizing committee had asked me to finish the show and skate last. The Russians put in a protest about it, saying that Rodnina always does skate last and that it was her privilege, but I really don't care where I skate in exhibitions. It does not make any difference to how I perform.

However, when I found out that I was going to have to follow them, it suddenly dawned that I had supposedly been put on a level with them and I had always regarded Rodnina as someone in a class on her own. So that was a new experience again, but it was one that I overcame and enjoyed. The pleasure lasted right through to the closing ceremony, which included a very disorganized version of a very bad chorus line comprising the eighteen medallists. It was great fun, with competitors from all the events having a good time together.

I was able to fly back from Gothenburg to London and meet my parents and my grandmother, who had driven up from Bristol to meet me at the airport. My parents had watched the European Championships on television, saving their vacation time and money for travelling to the Olympics. We spent the day and night with my brother Mark and sister-in-law June at their home in Roehampton, conveniently close to Heathrow Airport.

The following day, I was off to Denver again to try and forget all about the European win and concentrate on preparing for the Olympics. What happened at Lake Placid is recounted in the opening chapter, but I should like to add tribute here to Eileen Anderson, our Olympic team leader. She organized press conferences at times always convenient to me and saw to it that I was not exposed to undue pressure.

When I was having lunch in Lake Placid the day after the Olympic men's event had ended, a man came up and said that he had watched our short programmes on television and was so impressed with my performance that he decided he wanted to get tickets to watch the final free skating.

He bought three tickets for $1200 – $400 dollars (nearly £200) each – for himself, his wife and brother-in-law. His wife had told him he was crazy, but he took the trouble to come and tell me that it was all worth it because of the performance I had given.

That to me was icing on the cake, from someone I had never previously met and will probably never meet again, and from someone who had had no intention of being in Lake Placid for the figure skating and was in fact there for the ice hockey. It was surprising to know that tickets for a figure skating event, even from touts, would fetch that kind of money.

As people left Lake Placid when the Games were over, it was hardly the end for me. I had to buckle down again only three days later, to pull myself back to earth.

In March 1980, just three weeks after his Lake Placid triumph, Robin Cousins stood in Dortmund's luxurious Westfalenhalle stadium with the world at his feet, in more senses than one, hoping to win the triple crown success gained four years earlier by his compatriot, John Curry.

Whether Cousins was to win this week or not, he was already being followed by ice show impresarios and agents poised like vultures over their prey. It seemed highly unlikely that Robin would refuse the most suitable offer made after the World Championships.

As Olympic gold medallist and the world's best and most attractive exponent of high multiple jumps and sensational spins, his potential box-office value would be considerable, with or without the world title. But his heart was set on becoming the World Champion.

He ended the figures in an all-too-familiar situation, fifth, but in close touch with the four above him – Jan Hoffmann of East Germany, the two Americans, David Santee and Charlie Tickner, and a Frenchman, Jean-Christophe Simond.

The figures drawn were the same three as those in the Olympics, though starting each on the other foot. The rocker, which came first, was disappointing for Robin. His tracings were out of alignmnent and in consequence he scored fewer marks than he had hoped. Santee led the field after the rocker, with Hoffmann second and Tickner third.

Three of the nine judges at this point placed each of the top trio first, underlining how little there was between them. The second figure, the paragraph bracket, went better for the Englishman, who stayed fifth behind Simond while Hoffmann took over the lead and Tickner also passed the faltering Santee, who dropped to third.

The paragraph loop of Cousins did not get so many marks as he would have wished. Tickner erred and Santee rallied to move above him again to second spot.

In a nail-biting short free competition, Cousins was the last of the twenty-two competitors to skate and committed but one error, slipping near the end of his straight line step sequence. So good was his overall technique in spins and jumps that, despite the slip, he won the short free, seven of the nine judges awarding him 5·9 for presentation, so he rose two places to third behind Hoffmann, still in the lead, and Santee.

The two he overtook were Simond and Tickner. The Frenchman blew any medal chance he might have had, first when falling from his combination and later by jumping a single axel instead of a required double. Tickner, the 1978 champion, also failed his combination and moved down to fourth.

The long free skating will be long remembered. It had a silver lining for Cousins even though he was denied the title. The reason was simply that his figures were not quite good enough. The deficit still left when he began the long free proved just too great because Hoffmann did well enough to prevent the Olympic Champion from whittling away quite all the East German's initial advantage.

Due tribute must be paid to Hoffmann for possessing the all-round ability to cash in on that one weak chink in the Cousins armour.

That said, it should be emphasized beyond all shadow of doubt that Cousins, although only silver medallist this time on the overall rating, had proved throughout this and the two previous seasons to be easily and consistently the best free skater the world had seen.

More than that, his ultimate free skating performance at Dortmund was the best of his career and in a class joined only by Don Jackson of Canada in the less technically advanced days of 1962.

Cousins can be saluted for accomplishing a standard of jumps, spins and spirals of a quality, both technically and artistically, the like of which may not be matched by anyone in the foreseeable future.

What is more, his greatest achievements have been attained on what he himself describes as 'second-class knees,' referring to his two cartilage operations.

Hoffmann skated the best free performance of his life when he most needed it, though it suffered by comparison with Cousins, whose five triple jumps — two loops, two toe loops and a salchow — were merely the icing on a cake rich in flawless technique and presentation, justly meriting three sixes.

Cousins, in particular, would feel the irony if compulsory figures are soon removed from senior championships because, for three years, only the relative frailty of his figures denied the sport's outstanding free skater a world title.

Knowing that the next International Skating Union congress would consider a formal proposal to eliminate figures from senior international championships, its

Eamonn Andrews surprises Robin with an invitation to be the subject of *This is Your Life* for Thames Television in March 1980

president, Jacques Favart, predicted in Dortmund that figures are 'at death's door. They are a waste of time and prevent the skaters from being still more creative. That's my opinion. It will be for congress to decide.'

I arrived in Dortmund five days before the 1980 World Championships were due to begin, very much looking forward to what I knew was going to be my last competition and naturally hoping I could make it a good one.

I was well satisfied with the consistency of my skating, although I had to take a couple of days off because of 'flu – Olympic 'flu as we called it: we found out after Lake Placid that many of the competitors there had caught a similar virus.

It was something that Carlo was not particularly worried about. He seemed to think that the days off training might do me good and that the enforced rest could pay off. I felt well prepared and eager to compete again.

The figures which we drew were the same three and on the same foot as those

151

we had drawn in Gothenburg, so I was quite anxious to do them again as I knew I had been successful with them in Sweden.

An early morning start to the figures, seven o'clock, had me down on the ice in the first warm-up group. My first figure, the rocker, was probably not one of the better ones I had done in a long time, definitely not of the same standard as the equivalent figure I had done in the European Championships.

Mistakes which cost me precious tenths of a mark from most of the judges – not major mistakes, but silly ones that were unnecessary – had me in a position which I had hoped to avoid: fifth. So I knew that in the other two figures I was going to have to perform a lot better.

I had a long break in between the first and second figure, so went back to the hotel, had breakfast and managed to sleep for another hour. I returned to the rink as if I were starting again, completely fresh.

I had totally forgotten the disastrous mess I had made of the first figure and went out to trace the second possibly better than I had done before. I had skated a good paragraph bracket in Gothenburg, but believe this one was an improvement on that. The marks were accordingly better, so I felt that I had redeemed myself slightly.

The third figure, the change-edge loop, is not one that I particularly enjoy, but on this occasion I felt that my loops were as good as anyone else's. Thinking back, the figure that I normally do well I made a mess of and the ones which I normally do not do well were, by my standards, excellent.

In the three figures together, I felt that I averaged out a higher standard than I expected and I was pleased to think that my last figures in a championship were, in my opinion at least, collectively as good as I had ever done. The outcome, fifth, does not sound quite as good, but the fact is that the four above me all traced very good figures.

I was drawn last to skate in the short programme and felt confident of being able to skate it well. I had had an excellent practice in the morning and felt fine in the afternoon. I think most of the seven elements were the best of my life, particularly the jumps and spins.

But something I had never done before and would have been unlikely to do again was to trip up on a step sequence. It is nothing that you can guard against and, because of that, nothing that you could be particularly upset about – though, of course, I *was* upset and mad afterwards because it was a mistake that may have cost me the title.

But nobody can know that for certain. Had I skated a perfect short, then been under more pressure – who knows? – I might have had a bad long programme, so that kind of thing generally evens itself out. It was just one of those things and, as it happened, Hoffmann once more was 'Mr Consistent' and came out on top. I think he has proved to be probably the most consistent skater in modern times. Very rarely did one see him make a mistake that would be costly and seldom did he get flustered under pressure. Maybe that is because he had been in competitions long enough to know the ropes inside out, back to front and upside down. But I admired his technical skills and ability to win through under all circumstances.

That is something very important in an athlete of any kind and I think he has been someone for younger skaters to look up to as an example of how to conduct yourself through the turmoils of intense training and competition.

Going into the free skating, I knew that it was not going to depend on whether *I* skated well or badly. It very much depended on whether Jan skated well or badly. I knew that he was not one for making disastrous mistakes and knew that it would be easier for me to skate after him than to skate before him. We were drawn 'back to back', Jan skating second in the final group of six, and I third.

Jan skated very well and, when I saw his marks go up, I knew that it was impossible for me to win – because 6·2 was not a permitted mark! So I fully realized as I went on to the ice that there was no way that I could take this championship. I simply hoped that I could go out and perform for all the people who had travelled to see it. I mean, the support was incredible. The numbers from Bristol, Southampton and other English rinks and even from Scotland seemed to take the stadium by storm that night.

The atmosphere had been building up from Tuesday and, by Thursday night, along with a thousand or so from the British Army and their families at Dortmund garrison, not to mention my parents and gran, I felt almost as if I had been living in Dortmund all my life with the back-up I was getting from a crowd of 11,000 or 12,000, almost all of whom seemed to will me on.

In such circumstances, knowing I could not win but hoping I would make second, I really had to enjoy it and show everybody that it was possible to skate better than I had done at the Olympics. I know a lot of people said I should be happy with what I did at Lake Placid, but I knew that I could skate better and wanted to use this opportunity to prove it. I do not think I ever enjoyed a competition so much as the one in Dortmund.

The audience lifted me three feet off the ice with the opening bars of music and did not put me down again until I had finished and been given a most unbelievable reception.

I was upset to think that, whereas at Lake Placid I won without giving of my best, Jan did give of his best yet did not win. Yet here in Dortmund, we did the opposite. He skated superbly, though maybe not so well as he had at Lake Placid, and yet the positions were reversed, so perhaps that is the way it was meant to be.

But at least it was consoling to prove again that I was the world's top free skater and I went out on a note which for me was probably the ultimate – a performance which I do not believe I would ever be able to repeat. It was my personal best, and that is all that matters. Obviously one wants to win, but it is always a satisfying result when you are happy with what you have done and you know that it is better than you did the last time you went on the ice.

That is the way it should be. I knew as soon as I had finished the programme that I had done everything I had in my power to put over a good performance and to pull everything off without mistakes. I think Carlo and Christa were also very pleased, so that was enough for me.

We had added a couple of extra triples since the Olympic Games. I had two triple loops, two triple toe loops and a triple salchow, plus the usual double axels and other jumps, the spins and the steps.

Everything seemed to fall into place very easily and, with the five triples – the only time I had done more was in the 1976 Olympics at Innsbruck, when I included six – the quality of my skating I do not think had ever been better than it was in Dortmund. As I have said, I had been skating consistently during the run-up and Carlo had told me beforehand he was quite sure I was going to skate well because of the standard achieved during practice all that week.

I do not think I skated badly in the short programme, even with that fall. I looked back afterwards on the videos and felt very pleased with the overall reaction. I know a lot of people thought that I was a little disappointing in the Lake Placid Olympics, despite winning, because I did not do then all that some knew I could do. I think I proved to them, as well as to a lot more, that I could – and did – improve on it in Dortmund.

After Dortmund, the four-week ISU tour of World and Olympic medallists to fifteen European cities was rather an emotional experience as so many of us were planning to move on from the amateur championships circuit. The final performance, in Moscow on 10 April 1980, was one which I think many of us will long remember. It felt very strange to be skating together for the last time, having competed against each other so often for several seasons.

During that tour, I returned briefly to Bristol on 22 March for a civic reception of a kind I had hardly anticipated. I suppose I had not expected to receive such celebrity treatment so quickly. It was very difficult for me to accept that literally millions of people had seen on television what I had done during the previous two months.

The amount of enthusiasm and the number of people lining the streets of Bristol to welcome what they must have regarded as something of a triumphal homecoming was absolutely amazing as my open-topped 'bus of honour' paraded slowly amongst them.

It was an incredible day for myself, my whole family and, indeed, everyone involved, culminating in a big surprise by Eamonn Andrews as I became the

154

subject of the *This Is Your Life* television programme.

I was standing on the platform with the Lord Mayor, Tom Clarke, receiving a presentation on behalf of the city of Bristol, when Eamonn Andrews crept up behind the two of us and tapped me on the shoulder. I believe the crowd were concentrating so much on the presentation that few among them had noticed Eamonn running across Bristol's College Green before making his dramatic approach.

It all happened so fast and my immediate reaction was, 'Oh God, I'm only twenty-two and already they're doing my life!' But, obviously it was a great surprise to me and I was very honoured to find myself the subject of what has long been a very prestigious programme.

Having decided to turn professional, I then had to choose where I would like to go and with which show. In the end, it wasn't that difficult. Among the offers I received, *Holiday on Ice* came up with an excellent proposition for me to perform for that company around Europe, including two months at London's Wembley Arena. If I had accepted the other ice shows which were interested, I would have had to spend more of the time travelling abroad and more or less the deciding factor was that, with *Holiday on Ice*, I should be able to skate for some of the time in my home country and thus maintain a close contact with my family.

I had been very much looking forward to a professional career and don't expect that my style of skating will change unduly. I assume I shall just have to gear myself to performing every night, as opposed to competition training every day, and I hope that audiences henceforth will enjoy what I do as much as I enjoy doing it.

It's very hard for myself and my parents to accept that I may now be earning a great deal of money. Up to now we have always been thinking in pounds and pence, and now we shall have to think perhaps in terms of hundreds and thousands. I know it will be a great thrill for me to return some of my first pay cheques to my parents. For a long while they have been hoping to move. Helping to pay for a house large enough for all my family to be able to visit at the same time would, I believe, be some way to repay them for all the hard work and support they have given through the past years.

On 14 June 1980, the outstanding achievements of Robin Cousins were duly recognized in the Queen's Birthday Honours List with the award of the Medal of the British Empire 'for services to ice skating' – a fitting accolade for a truly remarkable young man.

APPENDIX 1

National and International Record

YEAR	VENUE	EVENT	FIGURES	FREE	OVERALL
1972	Billingham	Junior British Championship	4	1	1
	Richmond	British Championship	3	3	3
1973	Cologne	European Championship	18	14	15
	Calgary	Skate Canada	11	5	10
	Richmond	British Championship	2	2	2
1974	Zagreb	European Championship	16	6	11
	Kitchener	Skate Canada	10	3	6
	Richmond	British Championship	2	2	2
1975	Copenhagen	European Championship	11	8	11
	Colorado Springs	World Championship	15	11	12
	Johannesburg	Skate Safari	2	1	2
	Richmond	British Championship	2	1	2
1976	Geneva	European Championship	13	4	6
	Innsbruck	Winter Olympic Games	14	8	10
	Gothenburg	World Championship	14	8	9
	Ottawa	Skate Canada	4	2	2
	Richmond	British Championship	1	1	1
1977	Helsinki	European Championship	7	2	3
	Tokyo	World Championship	10	retired	
	Moncton	Skate Canada	2	1	1
	Richmond	British Championship	2	1	1
1978	Strasbourg	European Championship	5	1	3
	Ottawa	World Championship	4	1	3
	Richmond	British Championship	1	1	1
1979	Zagreb	European Championship	6	1	3
	Vienna	World Championship	5	1	2
	Richmond	Rotary Watches International	1	1	1
	Richmond	British Championship	1	1	1
	Tokyo	NHK International Trophy (free skating)	–	1	1
	The Hague	Ennia Challenge Cup (free skating)	–	1	1
1980	Gothenburg	European Championship	3	1	1
	Lake Placid	Winter Olympic Games	4	1	1
	Dortmund	World Championship	5	1	2

APPENDIX 2

How the Judges Mark

A figure skating championship is divided into three sections – compulsory figures, short free skating and long free skating. The marks for each section are added (and factorized where necessary) so that the figures are worth thirty per cent of the total marks, the short free is worth twenty per cent and the other fifty per cent is given to the long free skating.

The compulsory figures comprise three in number and the group of three is drawn the night before the championship from any of three groups, also the foot (*i.e.* left or right) on which each figure is begun.

In senior international championships there are normally nine judges. One set of marks is given by each judge for each figure. The maximum is six and decimal tenths are included. More than 4·5 is rarely awarded for a figure.

The short free skating comprises seven obligatory elements (*e.g.* specific jumps, spins and step sequences), to be completed within two minutes. For this, each judge awards two sets of marks up to six, for required elements and for presentation.

The long free skating is of five minutes' duration for men, with each competitor free to include whatever he likes, in any sequence, and to his own choice of music. For this again, the judges award two sets of marks up to six, for technical merit and for artistic presentation.

The totals of marks given offer good guidance to each skater's relative merits, but these are not the deciding factor. The result is determined by what is called the majority placings system.

By this method, the overall position in which a skater is put by each judge is enumerated and a skater's final placing is determined by the position in which a *majority* of judges place him.

When no skater has a majority for a particular place, *i.e.* when the issue is very close, it is difficult for the onlooker to assess the result and computers are used to work it out.

Examples of close finishes and how the final order is determined are given elsewhere in this book, with particular reference to the World Championships of 1978 in Ottawa and the European Championships of 1979 in Zagreb.

APPENDIX 3

Jumps and their Values

The following list describes which blade edges are used for take-offs and landings for each jump and the number of mid-air 360-degree revolutions each involves. The International Skating Union factor reflects the official recognition of difficulty. Thus, the higher the factor, the more marks a correctly performed jump merits in competition. Abbreviations used are:

f	forward	n	natural rotation
b	backward	r	reverse rotation
i	inside	TA	toe-assisted take-off
o	outside		

JUMP	TAKE-OFF	LANDING	REVOLUTIONS	DIRECTION OF ROTATION	ISU FACTOR
Axel Paulsen	fo	bo on opposite foot	$1\frac{1}{2}$	n	3
Double Axel Paulsen	fo	bo on opposite foot	$2\frac{1}{2}$	n	6
One foot Axel Paulsen	fo	bi on same foot	$1\frac{1}{2}$	n	3
Double one foot Axel Paulsen	fo	bi on same foot	$2\frac{1}{2}$	n	6
Inside Axel Paulsen	n	bo on same foot	$1\frac{1}{2}$	n	3
Double inside Axel Paulsen	fi	bo on same foot	$2\frac{1}{2}$	n	7
Triple inside Axel Paulsen	fi	bo on same foot	$3\frac{1}{2}$	n	10*
Loop	bo	bo on same foot	1	n	2
Double loop	bo	bo on same foot	2	n	5
Triple loop	bo	bo on same foot	3	n	8
Half loop	bo	bi on opposite foot	1	n	2
Double half loop	bo	bi on opposite foot	2	n	4
Toe loop	boTA	bo on same foot	1	n	2
Double toe loop	boTA	bo on same foot	2	n	4

* The triple inside Axel Paulsen factor is estimated

JUMP	TAKE-OFF	LANDING	REVOLUTIONS	DIRECTION OF ROTATION	ISU FACTOR
Triple toe loop	boTA	bo on same foot	3	n	8
Lutz	boTA	bo on opposite foot	1	r	3
Double lutz	boTA	bo on opposite foot	2	r	6
Triple lutz	boTA	bo on opposite foot	3	r	8
One foot lutz	boTA	bi on same foot	1	r	3
Double one foot lutz	boTA	bi on same foot	2	r	6
Toeless lutz	bo	bo on opposite foot	1	r	3
Double toeless lutz	bo	bo on opposite foot	2	r	8
Salchow	bi	bo on opposite foot	1	n	2
Double salchow	bi	bo on opposite foot	2	n	4
Triple salchow	bi	bo on opposite foot	3	n	7
One foot salchow	bi	bi on same foot	1	n	2
Double one foot salchow	bi	bi on same foot	2	n	4
Toe salchow	biTA	bo on opposite foot	1	n	2
Double toe salchow	biTA	bo on opposite foot	2	n	5
Walley	bi	bo on same foot	1	r	3
Toe walley	biTA	bo on same foot	1	r	2
Double toe walley	biTA	bo on same foot	2	r	5

PHOTO ACKNOWLEDGEMENTS

The authors and the publisher would like to thank the following for the use of copyright photographs: *Bristol Evening Post*, Bristol United Press, Colorsport, Gerald Dalton, Tony Duffy/All-Sport, Foto-Call, D. B. Gardner, Lehtikuva Oy, Don Morley/All-Sport, Steve Powell/All-Sport and *Skate Magazine*. Colour photograph of Robin Cousins preparing for an exhibition by Dan L. Hayward; all others by Tony Duffy/All-Sport.